AF753781

# STATE AND LOCAL GOVERNMENT IN THE UNITED STATES

# STATE AND LOCAL GOVERNMENT IN THE UNITED STATES

**M.H. TIMM (EDITOR)**

**Nova Science Publishers, Inc.**
*Huntington, New York*

**Senior Editors:** Susan Boriotti and Donna Dennis
**Coordinating Editor:** Tatiana Shohov
**Office Manager:** Annette Hellinger
**Graphics:** Wanda Serrano
**Book Production:** Matthew Kozlowski, Jonathan Rose and Jennifer Vogt
**Circulation:** Cathy DeGregory, Ave Maria Gonzalez, Ron Hedges and Andre Tillman

*Library of Congress Cataloging-in-Publication Data*
*Available Upon Request*

ISBN 1-59033-045-5.

Copyright © 2001 by Nova Science Publishers, Inc.
227 Main Street, Suite 100
Huntington, New York 11743
Tele. 631-424-NOVA (6682) Fax 631-425-5933
E Mail: Novascience@earthlink.net

All rights reserved. No part of this book may be reproduced, stored in a retrieval system or transmitted in any form or by any means: electronic, electrostatic, magnetic, tape, mechanical photocopying, recording or otherwise without permission from the publishers.

The authors and publisher have taken care in preparation of this book, but make no expressed or implied warranty of any kind and assume no responsibility for any errors or omissions. No liability is assumed for incidental or consequential damages in connection with or arising out of information contained in this book.

This publication is designed to provide accurate and authoritative information with regard to the subject matter covered herein. It is sold with the clear understanding that the publisher is not engaged in rendering legal or any other professional services. If legal or any other expert assistance is required, the services of a competent person should be sought. FROM A DECLARATION OF PARTICIPANTS JOINTLY ADOPTED BY A COMMITTEE OF THE AMERICAN BAR ASSOCIATION AND A COMMITTEE OF PUBLISHERS.

*Printed in the United States of America*

# CONTENTS

# PREFACE

The federal government is not the "be all and end all" of the United States' governing system. Many of the services we as citizens take for granted -- pensions and business development for example -- come from state and local governments. Ostensibly, this country operates under a federal system in which fifty separate entities share power, and those states were meant to hold a great deal of power, as they are closer to the people than is the central government in Washington. And, by extension, local governments are even nearer to the citizens than the states. The federal government, via grants and other types of funding, assists the sub-national governments in performing their duties, but cannot function without the support of the states. Tip O'Neill once said that "all politics is local;" therefore, understanding the state and local government processes is critical to being an informed citizen and voter.

This book presents a series of chapters reporting on the history and current operations of the state and local systems. Included are discussions on the statehood process, the application of federal labor laws to state employees, and how states operate pension plans and aid economic development. Several chapters also trace the federal money trail from Washington to the state and local level.

Jonathan T. Rose
August 29, 2001

# STATEHOOD PROCESS OF THE FIFTY STATES

*Garrine P. Laney*

## INTRODUCTION

After declaring its independence from Great Britain, a major issue facing the United States was disposal of lands located outside of colonial borders (crown lands). Proposals on the disposition of these western lands were discussed and, after much debate, the states decided to cede them to the Continental Congress. Several pieces of legislation considered by the Continental Congress shaped the process of admitting territories and other areas in to the Union. Among them, the Ordinance of 1787 provided for a statehood process that has served as a basic model for entities seeking to become states – creation of a territorial government, the presence of a delegate in the Continental Congress, and finally admission into the Union.

Article IV, Section 3 of the Constitution empowers Congress to establish rules and procedures for the admission of territories to statehood. Over the years, the statehood process has been refined as the federal Congress has addressed problems associated with becoming a state (such as shadow representation and non-English speaking populations, among others). Generally, the process requires that inhabitants of the territory propose a republican state constitution and government, that a majority of the electorate want statehood, and that the proposed new state have sufficient population and resources to support state government and to support its share of the federal government.

Traditionally, once their population reaches the required number, incorporated territories become states by petitioning Congress for admission to the Union. If Congress is so inclined, it passes an enabling act, which authorizes the people to write a state constitution. When the populace ratifies the state constitution, it is submitted to Congress for approval. If it is acceptable to both the House and the Senate, then Congress passes a joint resolution declaring the area a state. The statehood process is complete when the President signs the congressional resolution.

Some areas, however, used different strategies to become states. Several, such as Maine and Vermont, were parts of other states and lacked territorial status before admission to the Union. Some areas, such as Arkansas and Wyoming, called constitutional conventions without Federal authority; others followed Tennessee's example and not only called constitutional conventions but also elected "shadow" Senators and Representatives to Congress before statehood was granted. One – Texas – was an independent nation, while others, such as California and New Mexico, were military districts.

A table identifies the date each territory or other area sought to become a state, its date of admission, its date of referendum, how long it took, and any notable events that occurred during the statehood process.

## CONTINENTAL CONGRESS

After the thirteen American colonies declared their independence in 1776, some of them laid conflicting claims to the unoccupied territory west of the Appalachian Mountains belonging to Great Britain (crown lands). For example, Georgia and North Carolina claimed their western boundaries extended to the Mississippi River. Both Connecticut and Virginia claimed the territory northwest of the Ohio River. States that did no claim crown lands opposed ownership of them by individual states, primarily because they felt that national resources should not be used to protect and develop these lands that would benefit only a few.[1]

Several proposals were offered on how to dispose of crown or western lands. Among them was a suggestion that Congress be given the crown lands, "reserving to the states within whose limits such crown lands may be the entire and complete jurisdiction thereof."[2] Another proposal was that Congress use either the whole or part of the western lands for revenue purposes to defray the cost of the War, but allowing states with claims to western lands to maintain jurisdiction. Anticipating trouble over ownership of western lands, the Continental Congress in 1779 passed a resolution recommending that all such claims cease. Ratification of the Articles of Confederation was delayed until the states resolved the issued of the disposal of their western lands. Virginia, New York, Massachusetts and Connecticut ceded the soil and jurisdiction of the territory northwest of the Ohio River to the United States on the condition that new states be formed with the land. Although a large part of territory west of the Alleghenies remained unceded to Congress, it was expected that the other states would do so.[3]

The Continental Congress then turned to the issue of governance of the western lands that had been ceded. In 1780, the Continental Congress resolved that any land ceded to the national government would "be settled and formed into distinct republican states, which shall become members of the federal union, have the same rights to sovereignty,

[1] Douglas, Edward M. *Boundaries, Areas, Geographic Centers and Altitudes of the United States and the Several States*, Washington, Government Printing Office, 1932, p. 63-67.

[2] *Journals of the American Congress: From 1774-1788*, v. 2, June 23, 1778, p. 601.

[3] Alden George H., The Evolution of the American System of Forming and Admitting New States into the Union, *Annals of the American Academy of Political and Social Science*, November, 1901, v. 28, No. 3, p. 469-71; Douglas, *Boundaries, Areas, Geographic Centers*, p. 63-67; *Journals of Congress*, v. 3, October 30, 1779, p. 384-85.

freedom and independence as the other states."[4] It also provided that each state be not less than 100 nor more than 150 miles square. Two years later, an attempt was made to limit new states to a maximum of 130 miles square. Other suggestions on how to create new states were offered and probably influenced the methods pursued by Congress. A congressional committee, formed in 1783 to devise a plan of organization and government for the territory, produced a plan for a temporary government of the western territory (the Ordinance of 1784).[5]

## ORDINANCE OF 1784

The Ordinance of 1784 stated that, after the free population reached 20,000, a prospective state could hold its own convention at a time and place set by Congress. Initially, the district would use the constitution of one of the older states, but on attaining statehood, the new state legislature could amend the constitution or adopt its own. Prior to admission, a territory could send a delegate to Congress, who would have the right to debate, but not to vote. Only after free inhabitants in the territory numbered as many as the least numerous of the thirteen original states could they pursue statehood and if successful, enjoy full congressional representation. At first, the consent of nine states was necessary for admission, but this provision was amended to read "Provided the consent of so many states in Congress is first obtained as may at the time be competent to such admission."[6]

## ORDINANCE OF 1787

Evidently there was dissatisfaction with the Ordinance of 1784, for three years later, it was repealed. After considering a number of proposals, the Continental Congress passed An Ordinance for the Government of the Territory of the United States, Northwest of the River Ohio (the Ordinance of 1787), which provided for the creation of at least three but not more than five new states. Besides arranging for territorial government, the Ordinance established steps for admission of a territory to statehood. According to provisions of the Ordinance, once the territory's population reached sixty thousand free men, Congress could admit it to statehood on an equal footing with the original states, in all respects, provided that the permanent state constitution and government were republican in nature and conformed to the principles of the articles of the Ordinance, and that the new state could contribute its share of revenue to the Federal treasury. During this temporary territorial period, the legislature (composed of a legislative council and a

---

[4] *Journals of Congress*, v. 3, October 13, 1780, p. 535.

[5] Ibid., p. 474-75; *Journals of Congress*, v. 4, October 15, 1783, p. 296.

[6] Ibid., p. 476; *Journals of Congress*, v. 4, April 2, 1784, p. 373-380.

house of representatives) would elect a delegate to Congress who would have a seat in Congress with the right to debate but not to vote.[7]

## FEDERAL CONGRESS

Article IV, Section 3 of the new Constitution, adopted on September 13, 1788, vests Congress with authority for admitting new states into the Union. Other than prohibiting the formation of any new state within the jurisdiction of any other state, or the creation of any new state by combining two or more states or parts of states without the consent of the legislatures of states concerned as well as of Congress, the Constitution does not define specific conditions for statehood. Congress, therefore, is free to determine statehood admission requirements. In deciding if a territory should become a state, Congress has been influenced by political partisanship, the language of territorial residents, the size and ethnicity of a territory's population, regional and economic considerations, and various other issues. With time, Congress has developed certain standards and procedures for the admission of new states. Congress requires that inhabitants of the proposed new state believe in the principles of republican government; that a majority of the electorate desire statehood; and that the proposed new state have sufficient population and resources to support state government and to provide its share of the costs of the federal government.[8]

Many states joined the Union by following the tradition established by the Ordinance of 1787. That is, when residents of a territory show that they favor statehood, they can petition Congress through their territorial legislature or territorial delegate to Congress, or both, requesting admission to the Union. Congress considers the petition and, if favorably disposed, passes an enabling act authorizing the people, through a constitutional convention, to draw up a state constitution. The constitution has to be ratified by popular vote and then submitted to Congress for approval. If Congress finds it acceptable, the Senate and the House pass a joint resolution declaring the area a state. After the President signs the congressional resolution approving admission, the statehood process is complete.[9]

---

[7] *Journals of Congress*, v. 4, July 13, 1787, p. 751-54; Alden, *The Evolution of the American System of Forming and Admitting New States into the Union*, p. 476-78.

[8] U.S. Library of Congress. Congressional Research Service. Admission of States into the Union: A Brief Summary of Procedures. Report by William R. Tansill. Washington, 1970, p. 1-4; Ellis, Ulrich, *Formation of New States by Irregular Means*, Grafton, Australia, New England New State Movement, 1961, p. 2.

[9] University of Hawaii, Legislative Reference Bureau, Territory of Hawaii, *Procedures Followed by States Admitted into the Union without Congressional Enabling Acts*, Honolulu, The Bureau, February 1949, p. 1.

## NON-TRADITIONAL MEANS OF ADMISSION

A number of areas, however, used different strategies to achieve statehood.[10] Four areas were parts of other states and did not have territorial status before admission to the Union; they were admitted to the Union as separate entities by simple acts of admission. These states were Kentucky (from Virginia),[11] Maine (from Massachusetts),[12] Vermont (from New York),[13] and West Virginia (from Virginia).[14] Seven territories or areas (Tennessee, Michigan, Iowa, California, Oregon, Kansas, and Alaska) elected "shadow" Senators and Representatives to Congress before statehood was granted.[15] Each area initiated constitutional conventions without federal authority. "State" constitutions were designed and ratified by referendum, and Senators and Representatives were elected prior to the submission of petitions for admission.[16]

Five territories (Arkansas, Florida, Wyoming, Idaho, and Hawaii)[17] also drafted state constitutions without prior federal authorization, but did not elect Senators or Representatives until after they had achieved statehood.[18]

---

[10] U.S. Library of Congress. Congressional Research Service. Statehood Plebiscites in the Territories of the United State: A Brief History and Analysis. Report by Peter B. Sheridan. Washington, 1980, p. 1-18.

[11] Swindler, William F., ed., *Sources and Documents of United States Constitutions*, Dobbs Ferry, New York, Oceana Publications, 1975, v. 4, p. 129-41.

[12] Ibid., v. 4, p. 298-314, 330-32; Banks, Ronald F., *Maine Becomes a State, The Movement to Separate Maine from Massachusetts, 1785-1828*, Middletown, Connecticut, Wesleyan University Press, 1970, p. 150-54, 184-88.

[13] Swindler, Sources and Documents, v. 9, p. 485-506; Thomas, Dana Lee, *The Story of American Statehood*, New York, Wilfred Funk, Inc., 1961, p. 27-28.

[14] Swindler, *Sources and Documents*, v. 10, p. 339-41, 362-63.

[15] Ibid., v. 8, p. 205-22; v. 9, p. 125-26, 136-40, 151; v. 5, 197-99, p. 217-18; and v. 1, p. 440-47, 460-63; v. 2, p. 422, 424, 428-30; Ramsey, J.G. M., *The Annals of Tennessee*, Knoxville, East Tennessee Historical Society, 1967, p. 47-78; Dunbar, Willis F., *Michigan: A History of the Wolverine State*. Grand Rapids, Michigan, William B. Eerdmans, 1965, p. 301-306, 314-316; Peterson, William J. *The Story of Iowa*. New York, Lewis Historical Publishing Co., 1942, v. 1, p. 336-40, 344-49; Federal Writers' Project, *California*, New York, 1967, p. 51-53; Bancroft, Hubert H. *History of Oregon*, v. 2, San Francisco, The History Co., 1890, p. 423-41; Tuttle, Charles R., *A New Centennial History of Kansas*, Madison, Wisconsin, Interstate Book Co., p. 432-37; Gruening, Ernest, *The State of Alaska*, New York, Random House, 1968, p. 336-50, 495-508.
For a detailed discussion of shadow representation, see: U.S. Library of Congress. Congressional Research Service. Shadow Representatives in Congress: History and Current Developments. Report by Garrine P. Laney. Washington, 1991.

[16] Ibid., p. 2; Ellis, Ulrich, *Formation of New States by Irregular Means*, p. 3; U.S. Library of Congress. Legislative Reference Service. Election of Congressional Delegations Prior to the According of Statehood. Report by William R. Tansill. Washington, 1956, p. 1-19.

[17] Swindler, *Sources and Documents*, v. 2, p. 315-16, v. 3, p. 120; Thomas, David Y., *Arkansas and Its People, A History, 1541-1930*, New York, The American Historical Society, Inc., 1938, p. 84-90; Cash, William T., *The Story of Florida*, v. 1, New York, The American Historical Society, 1938, p. 339-42, 350-52; Larson, Taft A., *History of Wyoming*, Lincoln, University of Nebraska, 1965, p. 243-61.

[18] University of Hawaii, *Procedures followed by States admitted into the Union without Congressional Enabling Acts*, p. 5; Grupo de Investigadores Puertorriquenos, *Breakthrough from Colonialism: An Interdisciplinary Study of Statehood*, Rio Piedras, Puerto Rico, Editorial de la Universidad de Puerto Rico, 1984, v. 2, p. 1220-24.

A few areas were not territories when they sought admission to the Union. Texas was an independent nation for nearly 10 years prior to annexation by the United States. Its enabling act was incorporated in the joint resolution of Congress approving annexation. California was a conquered military district. New Mexico was also a conquered military district when it sought admission, but Congress handled its initial petition for statehood differently. Because its proposed constitution prohibited slavery, congressional representatives of southern states opposed New Mexico's admission in 1850. Congress granted California statehood instead, and the status of New Mexico was changed from that of a conquered military district to a territory. New Mexico finally became a state on January 6, 1912.[19]

## LANGUAGE AS A FACTOR IN THE STATEHOOD PROCESS

Although not proscribed by the constitution, English has always been the language of the U.S. Government. Language became a topic of debate when five territories with large groups of non-English speakers sought admission to the Union. When Louisiana became a state (through the Louisiana Purchase), a sizable number of its residents spoke French or Spanish. In spite of some opposition of admitting Louisiana as a state, Congress passed an enabling act requiring that Louisiana's judicial and legislative proceedings be conducted "in the language in which the laws and the judicial and legislative proceedings of the United States are now published and conducted."[20]

Language concerns were expressed about the admission of Arizona and New Mexico to the Union as well. The majority population of these two territories, which were acquired by the Treaty of Guadalupe-Hidalgo, spoke Spanish only. Their enabling acts required that public school instruction be conducted in English and that state officers and legislators be proficient enough in reading, writing, and speaking English to conduct official business without the aid of an interpreter. Once a state, however, New Mexico's constitution requires that all state laws be published in both English and Spanish for 20 years, and thereafter as the state legislature requires.[21] While the Oklahoma Territory had a large Native American population that spoke a variety of languages, Oklahoma's enabling act called for public schools to be conducted in English, but did not preclude the teaching of other languages in public schools.[22] Hawaii's enabling act simply required that all legislative proceedings be conducted in English. Later, the Hawaiian constitution made English and Hawaiian the official languages of the state.[23]

[19] Swindler, *Sources and Documents*, v. 1, p. 243-44, 257-60, 440-47, 460-63; v. 7, p. 2, 11, 15-22, 129-34; Ellis, *Formation of New States by Irregular Means*, p. 3, 5-6.

[20] Swindler, *Sources and Documents*, v. 4A, #10, Enabling Act, February 20, 1811, p. 73-74; Act of Feb. 20, 1811, Ch. 21, 2 Stat 641 (1811).

[21] Ibid., v. 7, Enabling Act, p. 87, 89, 122-23; New Mexico State Constitution, Article 20, Section 12.

[22] Ibid., v. 8, Enabling Act, p. 76, 79-80.

[23] Ibid., v. 3, Enabling Act, p. 78-82, 90; Hawaii State Constitution, Article 15, Section 4.

The following table identifies the date a territory or other area sought admission to the Union, its date of admission, its date of referendum, and how long it took to become a state. Any notable events that occurred during its admission process are also listed.

**Table 1. Petitions for Statehood**

| Name of Territory or Area | Date petitioned for statehood | Date admitted to Union | Time elapsed | Date of referendum | Notes |
|---|---|---|---|---|---|
| 1. Alabama | Nov. 1818 | Dec. 14, 1819 | 1 yr., 1 month | None held | **Nov. 1818:** Territorial legislature/delegate petition for statehood.<br>**Mar. 2, 1819:** Enabling act passed. |
| 2. Alaska | Mar. 30, 1916 | Jan. 3, 1959 | 41 yrs., 10 months | 1945 | **1884:** Congress passed 1st Organic Act.<br>**1906:** A congressional bill would have created 3 Alaska states: one on Seward Peninsula; one running from the Aleutians to Southeastern, and one in the interior. Electorate ratified state constitution and 1st Delegate introduced 1st statehood bill.<br>**1912:** Congress passed 2nd Organic Act.<br>**1945:** Referendum held, approved statehood by 6,822 to 9,630.<br>**1923:** Southeast sought to secede from the rest of Alaska;<br>**Nov. 6:** Straw vote in Southeast communities approved secession by 1,344 to 89.<br>**1949:** Alaska Statehood Committee created by territorial legislature.<br>**1950:** House and Senate passed statehood bills. Gallup poll showed 81 percent for, 8 percent against and 11 percent no opinion on statehood.<br>**1955-1956:** Constitution drafted and Alaskans voted to adopt the "Tenn. Plan" and elected 2 Senators and 1 representative. These prematurely elected Members had to run for re-election once the territory was admitted into the Union; one chose not to run.<br>**Apr. 24, 1956:** Constitution ratified by vote of 17,173 to 8,060.<br>**1956 and 1958:** Statehood bills introduced.<br>**1958:** Suggestion that Alaska be made a commonwealth like Puerto Rico was defeated 60 to 24 in the Senate.<br>**Aug. 26, 1958:** Alaskans voted 40,452 to 8,010 for the immediate admission of Alaska to the Union. |
| 3. Arizona | Mar. 1892 | Feb. 14, 1912 | 19 yrs., 10 months | None Held | **1892:** House passed a statehood bill.<br>**1902:** Arizona defeated by popular vote a move to admit the territories of New Mexico and Arizona as a single state. President Taft |

**Table 1. Petitions for Statehood—Continued**

| Name of Territory or Area | Date petitioned for statehood | Date admitted to Union | Time elapsed | Date of referendum | Notes |
|---|---|---|---|---|---|
| | | | | | refused to approve statehood until the clause providing for the recall of judges was deleted.<br>**June 1910:** Enabling act passed. |
| 4. Arkansas | Jan. 4, 1836 | Jun. 15, 1836 | 5 months | None held | **1833:** Delegate proposed an enabling act in the House. The territorial legislature did not wait for Congress but drafted a constitution on its own initiative. It justified its action on 2 grounds: prior precedent (Kentucky in 1792 and Maine in 1820) and under provisions of the 1803 treaty with France acquiring the La. Territory, the U.S. was obliged to admit to statehood any territory organized within the purchase when its residents had the basic instruments of self-government.<br>**Mar. 1836:** Constitution delivered to Secretary of State. Attorney General B. Butler argued that the territory had acted within the constitutional privilege of peaceable assembly and that the calling of a convention was a reasonable action in preparing for statehood. Many Congressmen were upset by an accompanying ordinance adapted by the constitutional convention that proposed conditions Congress was to accept in the process of admitting the territory to statehood. Congress responded by adopting a retroactive enabling act.<br>**June 15, 1836, and with the Act of June 23:** Congress rejected, retained or modified provisions of the objectionable ordinance. |
| 5. California | Nov. 13, 1849 | Sept. 9, 1850 | 10 months | None held | California was a conquered military district, not a territory, when it sought statehood.<br>**Sept. 1, 1849:** Constitutional convention met.<br>**Nov. 13, 1849:** Shadow representative elected.<br>**Dec. 15, 1849:** Shadow senator elected. State constitution ratified by people. |
| 6. Colorado | 1863 | Aug. 1, 1876 | 13 yrs., 5 months | None held | **1863:** Territorial delegate introduced a statehood bill. |

**Table 1. Petitions for Statehood—Continued**

| Name of Territory or Area | Date petitioned for statehood | Date admitted to Union | Time elapsed | Date of referendum | Notes |
|---|---|---|---|---|---|
| | | | | | **Mar. 1864:** Enabling act passed.<br>**1864:** Constitution rejected by voters, 1,520 to 4,672.<br>**1865:** A second draft was approved 3,025 to 2,870.<br>**May 1866 and 1867:** Congress passed statehood measures twice, but President Johnson vetoed each one because the draft constitution differed substantially from the enabling statute.<br>**Dec. 1875:** State constitution drafted.<br>**1876:** Constitution ratified by electorate. |
| 7. Connecticut | An original colony | Jan. 9, 1788 | ----- | None held | ---- |
| 8. Delaware | An original colony | Dec. 7, 1787 | ----- | None held | ---- |
| 9. Florida | Dec. 3, 1838 | Mar. 3, 1845 | 7 yrs., 3 months | 1937 | **Apr. 1837:** A majority of the electorate voted for statehood.<br>**Dec. 1838:** State constitution drafted. |
| 10. Georgia | An original colony | Jan. 2, 1788 | ----- | None held | ---- |
| 11. Hawaii | 1903 | Aug. 21, 1959 | 56 yrs. | 1940 | **1893:** Hawaiian monarchy was overthrown.<br>**1898:** U.S. annexed Hawaii.<br>**1900:** Congress passed the Hawaiian Organic Act.<br>**1903:** Territorial delegate petitioned for statehood. Similar petitions were repeated in 1911 and biennially until WWI. Except for acts of introduction, no official notice was ever taken of these petitions.<br>**1915:** Statehood bill introduced.<br>**1920s:** Japanese population in Hawaii reached 42 percent, perceived as the "yellow menace."<br>**1932:** Congressional resolution offered to direct the territorial government by a High Commissioner sent to Hawaii from Washington. |

**Table 1. Petitions for Statehood—Continued**

| Name of Territory or Area | Date petitioned for statehood | Date admitted to Union | Time elapsed | Date of referendum | Notes |
|---|---|---|---|---|---|
| | | | | | **1933:** Bill introduced in Congress to alter the Organic Act and empower the President to appoint nonresidents to the most important positions in the territory (government, secretary, and the judiciary).<br>**Jan. 1935:** Delegate introduced statehood bill.<br>**1935:** An official government-supported campaign was organized—Hawaii Equal Rights Committee.<br>**Nov. 1940:** Plebiscite held, voters approved 46,174 to 22,428 (67%).<br>**1943:** Statehood bill introduced.<br>**1947:** Hawaii Statehood Commission created by legislature. 1947: 1st bill to pass House of Representatives; similar bills passed twice in next 3 years; no response from Senate.<br>**May 1949:** State constitution drafted.<br>**Nov. 1950:** Constitution ratified by electorate. Commonwealth status suggested by Representative Butler.<br>**1950:** State constitution approved 82,788 to 27,109.<br>**1953:** Senator Smathers suggested a plebescite to determine Hawaiian preference for Commonwealth or statehood status.<br>**1955:** Hawaiian House of Representatives passed a resolution asking Congress to grant Hawaiians "relief" from payment of federal taxes.<br>**1956:** Proposal for the immediate election of a territorial governor gained support as a compromise to statehood; however, the proposal was never formally approved.<br>**1958:** Gallup's Mainland Public opinion poll showed 9 to 1 in favor of statehood. |
| 12. Idaho | July 4, 1889 | July 3, 1890 | 1 yr. | None held | **July 1889:** State Constitution drafted.<br>**Nov. 1889:** Constitution ratified by electorate. |
| 13. Illinois | April 18, 1818 | Dec. 3, 1818 | 8 months | None held | **1818:** Congress passed enabling act.<br>**1818:** State constitution drafted. |
| 14. Indiana | Dec. 11, 1815 | Dec. 11, 1816 | 1 yr. | None held | **Dec. 11, 1815:** Territorial legislature petitioned for statehood. |

**Table 1. Petitions for Statehood—Continued**

| Name of Territory or Area | Date petitioned for statehood | Date admitted to Union | Time elapsed | Date of referendum | Notes |
|---|---|---|---|---|---|
| | | | | | **Apr. 19, 1816:** Congress passed enabling act. |
| 15. Iowa | Oct. 7, 1844 | Dec. 28, 1846 | 2 yrs., 2 months | None held | **1844:** People voted in favor of a constitutional convention. Congress rejected boundaries fixed by state constitution and suggested other boundaries, which voters rejected twice. Voters chose to remain a territory rather than give up the Missouri River as the western boundary.<br>**May 1846:** 2nd constitutional convention met; ratified by voters Aug 3, 1846.<br>**Oct. 26, 1846:** Shadow representative elected; a senate representative was not chosen immediately because of a voting deadlock in the General Assembly. |
| 16. Kansas | Dec. 15, 1855 | Jan. 29, 1861 | 5 yrs., 1 month | None held | **Oct 23, 1855:** Constitutional convention met at Topeka<br>**Dec. 1855:** Constitution ratified by voters, 15,951 to 4,891.<br>**Mar. 4, 1856:** Shadow senator selected.<br>**Oct. 1859:** Fourth constitution ratified by voters.<br>**April 1861:** Shadow senator elected. |
| 17. Kentucky | No territorial status before admission to Union | June 1, 1792 | ----- | 1790 | **April 1792:** Constitution formed; once part of Virginia, did not have territorial status before admission to the Union. Admitted to the Union as a separate entity by simple act of admission. Ten conventions were called for the purpose of separating from Virginia; the 1st met in Danville, Dec. 27, 1784; various factions demanded four different political status options. They were that Kentucky become an independent country, become a part of the Spanish Empire, remain a part of Virginia, or join the Union as an independent state. |
| 18. Louisiana | Feb. 20, 1811 | April 30, 1812 | 1 yr., 2 months | None held | **1810:** Eastern opponents of statehood for the Territory of Orleans charged that the admission of a state in which the inhabitants were foreigners and of doubtful allegiance was a menace to the Union; felt admission into Union was a violation of the Constitution. |

**Table 1. Petitions for Statehood—Continued**

| Name of Territory or Area | Date petitioned for statehood | Date admitted to Union | Time elapsed | Date of referendum | Notes |
|---|---|---|---|---|---|
| | | | | | **1808:** A new legal code, approved for the territory under the guidance of Governor W. Claiborne, combined Colonial, French and Spanish laws with elements of the Napoleonic Code. French and English legal language; Napoleonic Code retained. |
| 19. Maine | No territorial status before admission to Union | Mar. 15, 1820 | ------ | None held | ----- |
| 20. Maryland | An original colony | April 28, 1788 | ------ | None held | ----- |
| 21. Massachusetts | An original colony | Feb. 6, 1788 | ------ | None held | ----- |
| 22. Michigan | 1834 | Jan. 26, 1837 | 2 yrs., 3 months | 1833 | **1834:** Territorial legislature petitioned for statehood. Congress refused because of a boundary dispute with Ohio. Enabling bill introduced, Congress voted to lay the bill on the table.<br>**Oct. 5, 1835:** Shadow senators elected; votes at referendum on constitution ratified 6,299 to 1,359.<br>**Nov. 1835:** Shadow representative elected.<br>**Sept. 30, 1836:** Senate's compromise measure that Michigan relinquish its land claim to Ohio is rejected by delegates to the Convention of Assent.<br>**Dec. 15, 1836:** Democrats, on their own initiative, called a convention and assented to the compromise. Congress recognized this unofficial "state" legislature. Members-elected to Congress received $7,776 in "monetary compensation" from Congress long before they were formally seated. |

**Table 1. Petitions for Statehood—Continued**

| Name of Territory or Area | Date petitioned for statehood | Date admitted to Union | Time elapsed | Date of referendum | Notes |
|---|---|---|---|---|---|
| 23. Minnesota | Feb. 26, 1857 | May 11, 1858 | 1 yr., 3 months | None held | Democratic and Republican delegates refused to jointly draft a state constitution; compromise achieved by rival groups. Delegates refused to sign the draft if it also contained the names of the political opposition. Dispute was settled by printing the draft constitution on color coded paper.<br>**Oct. 13, 1857:** Electorate ratified the new constitution 30,055 to 571. Elected Senators and Representatives after passage of a constitution, but *before* the territory was allowed to become a state. |
| 24. Mississippi | July 7, 1817 | Dec. 10, 1817 | 5 months | None held | **Mar. 1817:** Enabling act passed by Congress. |
| 25. Missouri | Mar. 6, 1820 | Aug. 10, 1821 | 1 yr., 5 months | 1819 | **Mar. 1820:** Congress passed enabling act.<br>**June 1820:** State constitution drafted.<br>**Mar. 1821:** Congress passed resolution providing for admission of territory into the union on a certain condition.<br>**June 1821:** Missouri assents to condition of admission. Slavery an issue; enabling act passed with the promise that slavery be prohibited in the Louisiana Territory north of 36 degrees and 30 minutes north latitude and provided that the state legislature declare by "a solemn public act" that this offending clause (a law prohibiting free Blacks from setting within the state) would never be carried out. |
| 26. Montana | Jan. 14, 1884 | Nov. 8, 1889 | 5 yrs., 10 months | 1884 | **1884:** Constitution drafted and ratified by electorate. Congress *rejected* the 1884 constitution on the technicality that it had not been authorized by an enabling act passed first by Congress itself.<br>**Oct. 1889:** 2nd constitution and enabling act ratified by electorate. |
| 27. Nebraska | April 19, 1864 | Mar. 1, 1867 | 3 yrs., 1 month | 1860 & 1864 | **Mar. 1860:** 1st proposal for a constitutional convention was rejected by voters.<br>**April 1864:** Congress took the initiative and passed an enabling act without a demand by territorial residents; voters again defeated a proposal for a state convention. |

**Table 1. Petitions for Statehood—Continued**

| Name of Territory or Area | Date petitioned for statehood | Date admitted to Union | Time elapsed | Date of referendum | Notes |
|---|---|---|---|---|---|
| | | | | | **June 21, 1866:** Despite irregularities at the referendum election, the constitution carried by vote of 3,938 to 3,838. Consequently, the territorial Governor proposed in Jan. 1866, that legislators themselves draw up a constitution. Constitution lacked a provision for universal male suffrage, so the act of admission stipulated that the territory should adopt one as a "fundamental condition" of admission. President Johnson vetoed the bill of admission, citing the lack of adequate provision for deferring political and taxing authority. Congress overrode the veto. Johnson signed the proclamation of admission. |
| 28. Nevada | Mar. 21, 1864 | Oct. 31, 1864 | 7 months | None held | **Mar. 1864:** Congress passed enabling act; state constitution ratified by electorate. Vote result: 5,150 for statehood, 3,012 against it. |
| 29. New Hampshire | An original colony | June 21, 1788 | ------ | None held | ----- |
| 30. New Jersey | An original colony | Dec. 18, 1787 | ------ | None held | ----- |
| 31. New Mexico | June 20, 1850 | Jan. 6, 1912 | 61 yrs., 7 months | 1850 | **1850:** Constitutional convention drafted a state constitution; shadow senator and representative elected.<br>**Sept. 9, 1850:** Congress ignored the constitution and created territory of New Mexico. Statehood delayed for decades because of disputed Spanish and Mexican land titles, Indian uprisings, range wars and ethnic concerns. |
| 32. New York | An original colony | ------ | ----- | None held | ----- |
| 33. North Carolina | An original colony | ------ | ----- | None held | ----- |
| 34. North Dakota | Aug. 17, 1883 | Nov. 2, 1889 | 3 months | 1883 | Nearly every year a petition was sent to Congress requesting admission as two states.<br>**Feb. 22, 1889:** Enabling act passed. |

**Table 1. Petitions for Statehood—Continued**

| Name of Territory or Area | Date petitioned for statehood | Date admitted to Union | Time elapsed | Date of referendum | Notes |
|---|---|---|---|---|---|
| | | | | | **July 4, 1889:** Constitutional convention met.<br>**Aug. 1889:** Constitution drafted.<br>**Oct. 1, 1889:** Voters approved the proposed constitution. |
| 35. Ohio | April 30, 1802 | Mar. 1, 1803 | 11 months | 1802 | **April 1802:** Congress passed enabling act; Nov 8: second constitution drafted. |
| 36. Oklahoma | Oct. 14, 1905 | Nov. 16, 1907 | 2 yrs., 1 month | 1890 | **Oct. 1905:** Five civilized tribes called a convention, drafted a constitution for the proposed state of Sequoyah.<br>**June 1906:** Congress passed an enabling act; state constitution drafted. |
| 37. Oregon | Nov. 9, 1857 | Feb. 14, 1859 | 1 yr., 3 months | 1857 | **Nov. 9, 1857:** Voters at June 7 referendum ratified the constitution by a large majority, 7,195 to 3,215; however, by an even larger majority an article prohibiting the admission of free blacks into Oregon was approved. (This provision was not deleted from the constitution until 1926).<br>**1858:** Shadow senators and representatives elected. State constitution barred free blacks from the state. |
| 38. Pennsylvania | An original colony | Dec. 12, 1787 | ------ | None held | ----- |
| 39. Rhode Island | An original colony | May 29, 1790 | ------ | None held | ----- |
| 40. South Carolina | An original colony | May 23, 1788 | ------ | None held | ----- |
| 41. South Dakota | Sept. 4, 1883 | Nov. 2, 1889 | 6 yrs., 2 months | 1883 | **Sept. 1883:** State constitution drafted.<br>**Nov. 1883:** Constitution ratified by electorate.<br>**Feb. 1889:** Congress passed enabling act. |
| 42. Tennessee | Jan. 11, 1796 | June 1, 1796 | 4 months | 1796 | **Jan. 1796:** Petitioned for statehood. Congress delayed action so Tennessee organized a state government.<br>**May 29, 1796:** Legislature elected shadow senators.<br>**Mar. 28, 1796:** Shadow representatives elected. |

**Table 1. Petitions for Statehood—Continued**

| Name of Territory or Area | Date petitioned for statehood | Date admitted to Union | Time elapsed | Date of referendum | Notes |
|---|---|---|---|---|---|
| | | | | | **May 9, 1796:** Senators presented credentials but received as visitors only. Members-elect had to run for re-election once statehood was granted. |
| 43. Texas | No territorial status before to Union | Dec. 29, 1845 | ------ | None held | Was never a territory. Was an independent nation for nearly 10 years prior to annexation by the United States. It's "enabling act" was incorporated in the joint resolution of Congress approving annexation. |
| 44. Utah | Dec. 27, 1849 | Jan. 4, 1896 | 46 yrs., 11 months | None held | **Mar. 1849:** Constitution for "State of Deseret" was drafted and approved<br>**Dec. 27, 1849 and Jan. 28, 1850:** Memorial of State of Deseret presented to Senate and House Representatives, respectively.<br>**Jan. 23, 1862:** State Constitution drafted.<br>**Mar. 1862:** State constitution ratified by electorate. Territorial delegate petitioned Congress.<br>**July 1862:** "Senator-Elect" presents petition of Utah Territory for statehood.<br>**May 1895:** State constitution ratified by electorate. |
| 45. Vermont | No territorial status before admission to Union | ------ | ----- | None held | Functioned as an independent state for more than 13 years before achieving statehood.<br>**January 1791:** Vermont ratified the Constitution of the U.S.<br>**March 4, 1791:** Congress passed act admitting Vermont into the Union. |
| 46. Virginia | An original colony | June 25, 1788 | ------ | None held | ----- |
| 47. Washington | 1867 | Nov. 11, 1889 | 22 yrs. | None held | **1867:** Territorial delegate petitioned Congress for statehood.<br>**July 1878:** State constitution drafted.<br>**Feb. 1889:** Congress passed enabling act.<br>**Oct. 1889:** Constitution ratified by electorate. |

**Table 1. Petitions for Statehood—Continued**

| Name of Territory or Area | Date petitioned for statehood | Date admitted to Union | Time elapsed | Date of referendum | Notes |
|---|---|---|---|---|---|
| 48. West Virginia | No territorial status before admission to Union | June 20, 1863 | ------ | 1861 | Never a territory, was part of Virginia. When Virginia seceded from the Union a convention met on June 11, 1861 to reorganize the state government. Convention passed an ordinance for the election of a "lawful government." New state legislature elected and it elected Federal Senators to replace those expelled by Congress because of secession. State legislature created a new "state." At referendum on whether a new state constitution should be drafted, the electorate voted 28,489 to 781 in favor.<br>**Oct. 1861:** Referendum on whether to create a new state approved by voters 18,408 to 781.<br>**May 3, 1862:** Draft Constitution ratified 28,321 to 572. |
| 49. Wisconsin | Aug. 6, 1846 | May 29, 1848 | 1 yr., 9 months | None held | 1846: Congress passed enabling act.<br>**1847:** 1st constitution draft defeated.<br>**1848:** Constitution drafted and approved. |
| 50. Wyoming | Sept. 30, 1889 | July 10, 1890 | 10 months | None held | **Sept. 1889:** Constitution drafted. Nov. 1889: constitution ratified by electorate. |

## Sources

Adams, Ben. Hawaii, The Aloha State, Our Island Democracy in Text and Pictures. New York, Hill and Wang, 1959.

Alden, George H. The Evolution of the American System of Forming and Admitting New States into the Union. Annals of the American Academy of Political and Social Science. v. 28, No. 3, November, 1901: 469-478.

Bancroft, Hubert H. The Works of Hubert Howe Bancroft. San Francisco, The History Company, 1889: Vol. 26, History of Utah, 1850-1886.

Banks, Ronald F. Maine Becomes a State, The Movement to Separate Maine from Massachusetts, 1785-1828. Middletown, Connecticut, Wesleyan University Press. 1970.

Bell, Roger. Last Among Equals, Hawaiian Statehood and American Politics. Honolulu, University of Hawaii Press, 1984.

Bruno, Andorra and Garrine P. Laney. Political Development of U.S. Insular Areas. Washington, Congressional Research Service, Library of Congress, 1992. 39 p.

Dunbar, Willis F. Michigan: A History of the Wolverine State. Grand Rapids, Michigan, William B. Eerdmans Publishing Co. 1965.

Ellis, Ulrich. An Historical Survey of the Steps Taken Without Prior Parliamentary Authorization, Which Led to the Rapid Establishment of Seventeen of America's Fifty-Self-governing States. Grafton, New England New State Movement, 1961.

Federal Writers' Project of the Work Projects Administration for the State of California. California, A Guide to the Golden State. New York, Hastings House. 1967. (American Guide Series)

Federal Writers' Project of the Work Projects Administration for the State of Kansas. Kansas: A Guide to the Sunflower State. New York, Hastings House. 1949. (American Guide Series)

Federal Writers' Project of the Work Progress Administration for the State of Mississippi. Mississippi, A Guide to the Magnolia State. New York, Hastings House. 1949.

Federal Writers' Project of the Works Progress Administration for the State of Vermont. Vermont: A Guide to the Green Mountain State. Boston, Houghton Mifflin Co. 1968.

Federal Writers' Project of the Work Projects Administration for the State of Montana. Montana: A State Guide Book. New York, Hastings House. 1949. (American Guide Series)

Federal Writers' Project of the Works Progress Administration for the State of South Dakota. South Dakota: A Guide to the State. New York, Hastings House. 1952. (American Guide Series)

Federal Writers' Project of the Work Projects Administration for the State of Tennessee. Tennessee: A Guide to the State. New York, Hastings House, 1949. (American Guide Series)

Gruening, Ernest. The State of Alaska. New York, Random House, 1968.

Grupo de Investigadores Puertorriquenos. Breakthrough From Colonialism: An Interdisciplinary Study of Statehood. Rio Piedras, Puerto Rico, Editorial de la Universidad de Puerto Rico. 1984. 2 v.

Joesting, Edward. Hawaii, An Uncommon History. New York, W.W. Norton, Inc., 1972.

Jones, Thomas C., ed. The Hawaii Book: Story of Our Island Paradise. Chicago, Ferguson Pub. Co., 1961.

Journals of the American Congress: From 1774 to 1788,

Laney, Garrine P. Shadow Representatives in Congress: History and Current Developments. Washington, Congressional Research Service, 1991. 7 p.

Larson, Taft A. History of Wyoming. Lincoln, University of Nebraska Press. 1965.

Lavandero, Marcos Ramirez, ed. Documents on the Constitutional Relationship of Puerto Rico and the United States. Washington, Puerto Rico Federal Affairs Administration, 1988.

Lineberry, William P., ed. The New States: Alaska and Hawaii. New York, Wilson Co., 1963.

Naske, Claus-M. An Interpretative History of Alaskan Statehood. Anchorage, Alaska Northwest Pub. Co., 1973.

Neff, Andrew Love. History of Utah, 1847 to 1869. Salt Lake City, Utah, Deseret News Press, 1940.

Peterson, William J. The Story of Iowa. New York, Lewis Historical Pub. Co., 1952.

Ramsey, J.G.M. The Annals of Tennessee. Knoxville, East Tennessee Historical Society, 1967.

Swindler, William F., ed. Sources and Documents of United States Constitutions. Dobbs Ferry, New York, Oceana Publications, Inc., 1973. 10 v.

Sheridan, Peter B. Statehood Plebiscites in the Territories of the United States: A Brief History and Analysis. Washington, Congressional Research Service, 1980: 28p.

Tansill, William R. Election of Congressional Delegations Prior to the According of Statehood. Washington, Legislative Reference Service, Library of Congress, 1955. 19 p.

-----. Admission of States into the Union: A Brief Summary of Procedures. Washington, Congressional Research Service, 1970.

Thomas, Dana Lee. The Story of American Statehood. New York, Wilfred Funk, Inc., 1961.

Thomas, David Y. Arkansas and Its People, A History, 1541-1930. New York, The American Historical Society. 1938.

Thorpe, Francis N., ed. The Federal and State Constitutions Colonial Charters, and other Territories, and Colonies, Now or Heretofore Organic Laws of the States Forming the United States of America. Washington, G.P.O. Republished by Scholarly Press, Grosse Pointe, Michigan. 1909. 7 v.

Tuttle, Charles R. A New Centennial History of Kansas. Madison, Wisconsin, Interstate Book Co. 1876.

University of Hawaii, Legislative Reference Bureau, Territory of Hawaii. Procedures Followed by States Admitted into the Union Without Congressional Enabling Acts. Honolulu, The Bureau, February 15, 1949. 14 p. (Report no. 50-62883)

Workers of the Writers' Program of the Work Projects Administration in the state of Michigan. Michigan: A Guide to the Wolverine State. New York, Oxford University Press, 1941. (American Guide Series)

Workers of the Federal Writers' Project of the Works Progress Administration for the state of North Dakota. North Dakota: A Guide to the Northern Prairie State. New York, Oxford University Press. 1950. (American Guide Series)

Workers of the Writers' Program of the Work Projects Administration for the State of Utah. Utah: A Guide to the State. New York, Hastings House, 1945. (American Guide Series)

Workers of the Writers' Program of the Work Projects Administration in the State of Washington. The New Washington: A Guide to the Evergreen State. Portland, Oregon, Binfords & Mort, 1950. (American Guide Series)

Workers of the Writers' Program of the Work Projects Administration in the State of Wisconsin. Wisconsin: A Guide to the Badger State. New York, Hastings House, 1954. (American Guide Series)

Wormuth, Francis D. The Constitution and the Territories. Current History, v. 29, December 1955: 337-42.

Wright, Theon. The Disenchanted Isles, The Story of the Second Revolution in Hawaii. New York, The Dial Press, 1972.

Writers' Program of the Work Projects Administration in the State of Oregon. Oregon: End of the Trail. Portland, Binfords & Mort, 1940. (American Guide Series)

# State and Local Pension Plans: Economically Targeted Investments and Social Responsibility Screening

***Celinda Franco, Edward B. Rappaport and James R. Storey***

## Introduction

President Clinton has proposed to invest a portion of Social Security trust fund reserves in marketable securities as part of an initiative to improve that program's long-term financial outlook. One source of opposition to this idea stems from concern that pressures would lead to the allocation of Social Security assets in the securities markets among industries and firms based on political considerations.

This aspect of the Social Security reform debate has led policy makers to seek information on the investment policies of state and local government defined benefit pension plans. Because the success, or lack thereof, of these plans' investments are important to their electorates, managers have long been subject to political pressures regarding the allocation of investment dollars. In 1985, state and local plans held $1.4 trillion in assets, mostly invested in stocks (51%) and bonds (32%).[1] Other investments included real property, mortgages, and money market instruments. These assets constituted about one third of all assets held by employer pension plans in the United States and about one fifth of all U.S. investment capital.[2]

This report summarizes the recent literature regarding the ways in which the investment policies of state and local government pension plans have been shaped by non-financial considerations. First, the general considerations involved in pension plan financing are discussed. The laws that regulate the behavior of plan fiduciaries are then summarized. The nature of the external pressures on plan investment policies are

---

[1] CRS Report 98-774, *Pension Plans Sponsored by Employers: Summary of Major Trends*, James R. Storey. p. 5.

[2] Spencer's Research Reports. *Economically Targeted Investments Are Generally Limited to Government and Nonprofit Pension Plans*. October 17, 1997, p. 142-1.

discussed. Finally, the specific ways in which state and local plan investment policies have responded to these pressures are illustrated. This report does not attempt any independent assessment of the efficacy of these policies.

## BASIC PURPOSE OF PENSION PLAN INVESTING

Defined benefit (DB) pensions offer workers the prospect of future benefits, usually based on salary level, length of service, and attained age.[3] In most cases, the promised benefits will be paid decades into the future. To provide assurance that those future obligations will be adequately funded, and to smooth out the employer's pattern of contributions over time, moneys are invested far in advance of the expected benefit payouts. Whereas pensions were once informal, dependent only on the good faith of the employer, state and federal laws have evolved to the point that promised benefits have become a vested right and a legal obligation of the employer. To see that this obligation is met, rules regarding pre-funding and responsible management of plan assets have been developed.

Generally, each pension plan investment should be chosen to provide the best possible expected return for its level of risk, and overall risk must be limited to an appropriate level. The investment approach taken is generally conservative. There is little justification for a plan manager to undertake speculative investments if planned contributions have been made in a timely manner and the plan's sole objective is to accumulate assets sufficient to meet benefit payments.[4]

## LAWS REGULATING PENSION FUND INVESTMENT

The investment policies of all non-federal pension plans in the United States are subject, by law, to certain general principles, such as *prudence, loyalty, and diversification*. As interpreted by longstanding legal precedent, these principles are very exacting of trustees and other fiduciaries. Furthermore, statutory law provides criminal penalties for violation of fiduciary duties. The following is a general description of the laws that guide pension investment policies.

---

[3] Defined benefit pension plans often are referred to as DB plans. This report does not focus on investment policies of defined contribution (or DC) plans. DC plans accumulate assets in individual accounts for each participant. Participants often have some control over the manner in which their funds are invested. Hence, the assets of DC plans are not subject to the possibilities of politically motivated allocation decisions in the way that the group-managed assets of DB plans may be.

[4] Better-than-expected returns may inure ultimately to the benefit of the plan sponsor, but there are legal limits to the recapture of "excess" assets by private-sector sponsors. In any case, the trustees' legal obligation is to act solely in the interest of beneficiaries. "Recapture" may occur indirectly, however, by a sponsor's reducing future plan contributions in recognition of good investment performance.

## Employee Retirement Income Security Act and State Trust Laws

The Employee Retirement Income Security Act of 1974 (ERISA) (P.L. 93-406) regulates employer-sponsored benefit plans in the private sector. Although Title I, which includes the rules for fiduciary conduct, does not apply to state and local plans, ERISA's concepts regarding investment policy are similar to those of state law and common law antecedents. ERISA requires that plan assets be invested with adequate diversification and "with the care, skill, prudence, and diligence under the circumstances then prevailing that a prudent man acting in a like capacity and familiar with such matters would use..." The duty of *loyalty* requires that "A fiduciary shall discharge his responsibilities with respect to a plan solely in the interest of participants and beneficiaries and for the exclusive purpose of providing benefits...and defraying reasonable expenses."

These ERISA principles were derived from the body of state trust laws, which in turn were based on common law. Legal scholars differ on whether the concept of prudence in ERISA holds fiduciaries to a higher standard than under the general law of trusts, but the general principles are well established and apply to state and local plans, even though Title I of ERISA does not.

The concept of prudence has evolved somewhat in recent decades, however. Formerly, state trust laws specified exclusive *legal lists* of permissible asset categories, and these lists generally included only the safest investments, such as investment-grade bonds. Essentially, prudence was interpreted as diligent avoidance of almost all risk. However, under the current concept, some risk can be undertaken consciously to achieve a higher potential return, if the expected return is as favorable as possible commensurate with the risk, and if the portfolio is adequately *diversified.*[5]

When ERISA was enacted in 1974, plans of state and local governments and various nonprofit organizations (such as churches) were excluded from most of that law's pension rules for several reasons. First, insolvencies of DB plans and plan terminations have been rare in the public sector, and, on those few occasions, beneficiaries have experienced only temporary interruptions of payments.[6] Second, the personal financial interest in pension plans on the part of public officials is less significant than is often the case for owners and executives of profit-making firms. Finally, the constitutionality of the federal government's regulating state and local government plans is at least debatable.

---

[5] According to modern portfolio theory, diversification is not just a matte of limiting the size of individual investments but is enhanced if the returns of the various investments are *negatively correlated.* That is, returns on some investments will tend to increase in value when returns on others are declining.

[6] Because most public plans do not fully pre-fund their liabilities, there is always the possibility of problems arising in the future, especially if governments should reduce their workforce size while still servicing large numbers of retirees. However, a government's taxing power distinguishes the nature of this problem form that facing financially troubled firms in the private sector.

## U.S. Internal Revenue Code

Public as well as private plans must comply with a number of requirements in order to receive the tax benefits of §401(a) of the U.S. Internal Revenue Code. The plan's assets must be maintained in a trust for the exclusive benefit of participants and beneficiaries. Prudent investor standards apply, and the plan must not pay more than fair market value when purchasing assets. In particular, pursuant to self-dealing prohibitions, funds cannot be lent to the plan sponsor without adequate security or a reasonable rate of return, nor can securities be purchased there from for more than adequate consideration.[7]

Tax law thus provides another benchmark for proper pension trusteeship, but its practical significance in the case of public funds is blunted by the fact that state and local governments do not pay income tax. A primary sanction for violation would be the revocation of a plan's tax-exempt status, but this action would be of no direct consequence to a public agency. The other sanction available is to tax participants on their benefits as they accrue in the current year rather than to defer taxation to later years when benefits are paid, a consequence that could affect the sanctioned government indirectly by generating political discontent within its workforce and, perhaps, its electorate.

# NON-FINANCIAL INFLUENCE ON INVESTMENT POLICIES

Pressure is often felt by pension plan trustees and managers in both the public and private sectors to use a fund's assets to pursue objectives that are ancillary to the primary purpose of assuring that pension liabilities can be paid when due. These ancillary objectives are often grouped into two categories: *economically targeted investments* (ETIs) of pension funds, intended to boost the economic well-being of an industry, population group, or geographic area that ETI advocates seek to help; and *social responsibility screens* of pension investments, designed to withhold capital from a firm, industry or government that engages in activities that screening advocates want to discourage, or to overweight a portfolio with investments in firms that advocates want to encourage.

An ETI is an investment undertaken (1) to achieve a specific economic benefit (such as job creation or homebuilding) that is (2) of value to some important population group in the jurisdiction that supports the pension plan while (3) still earning a market rate of return. This intention to seek investments that pay a market rate of return distinguishes ETIs from social responsibility screens. Screening usually does not point managers toward specific investments but instead modifies the universe of securities from which investments are selected. A recent example of an ETI is an investment in the development of a statewide network of golf courses by the state of Alabama's employee

[7] A special legislative exemption from the exclusive benefit and prohibited transaction rules was needed for state and local pension funds in New York to buy special securities for the financial rescue of New York City in 1976.

pension fund to promote tourism. An example of social responsibility screening was the widespread use of portfolio screens by both public and private plans to stocks of certain companies doing business in South Africa when racial apartheid was official policy in that country.

Foes of ETIs and screening oppose them in part on the belief that governments should not act to distort the allocation of capital that the private markets produce. They also oppose these policies specifically as violations of the legal principle that plan fiduciaries must act solely in the interest of participants and beneficiaries.

Advocates for ETIs and social responsibility screens maintain that such policies do not detract from a plan manager's primary purpose of achieving the best economic return possible at an acceptable level of financial risk. Nevertheless, the fiduciary duties required by ERISA and related state laws can narrow considerably the scope allowed for social responsibility screening and ETIs, so much so that some argue the scope to be virtually vanishing. If an investment manager has single-mindedly sought out the most advantageous investments on behalf of participants, desirable social effects, if any, would seem to be coincidental. However, the claim is made for ETIs that they can provide returns at least as good as returns on the investments for which they would be substitutes. Regardless of what the impact of ETIs and investment screens may be on rates of return, the overall performance of public pension managers has been comparable to that of private fund managers. A 10-year study by Wilshire Associates that compared the investment performance of 50 large corporate pension funds with that of 50 large public plan funds found a 12.3% annual rate of return for the private funds and an 11.4% return for the public fund. This entire difference was attributable to a higher risk level in the asset allocation strategies of the private funds.[8]

Excellent investment performance is less often claimed for social investing generally, but arguments are made for the application of negative screens to relatively narrow investment categories (for example, the exclusion of tobacco firms from a plan's portfolio). Exclusion of the stock of a small number of firms leaves a large universe of other firms still to be chosen, thereby resulting in little change in portfolio performance compared to that of an unscreened portfolio. It is further argued by advocates of screening that a manufacturer whose product or manufacturing process imposes large social costs eventually will encounter major legal and political problems that may result in financial difficulty. Prices in financial markets ultimately will reflect such difficulty. An index of 400 stocks of companies acceptable in most socially screened portfolios (the Domini 400Social Index) did achieve a total return for the period 1991-1997 that exceeded returns for the S&P 500, a commonly used benchmark of stock market performance.[9]

---

[8] Pension and Benefits Reporter. *Public Pension Funds Defended as Social Security Debate Continues.* Bureau of National Affairs, Inc. Washington, DC. March 8, 1999. p. 683.

[9] Spencer's Research Reports. *Socially Responsible Investing Largely Limited to Screened Stock Portfolios.* Charles D. Spencer & Associates, Inc. Chicago, IL. August 7, 1998. p. 142-7.

## Federal Advisories on ETIs and Social Responsibility Screens

The notion of ETIs increased in appeal in the early 1980s and led to controversy in Congress as some Members felt that ETIs would threaten the adequacy of pension funding. The U.S. Department of Labor (DoL) addressed this controversy in 1994 by issuing Interpretive Bulletin No. 94-1 for pension plans under its jurisdiction. DoL stated that ETIs are acceptable under ERISA if expected rates of return are commensurate with those of other investments with similar risk characteristics. At the same time, DoL indicated that some leeway could be allowed in an ETI's meeting this test for ETIs with features that make such advance assessments difficult.[10]

In a 1998 advisory opinion,[11] DoL addresses the question of a pension plan including "socially responsible funds" and reached a similar conclusion. That is, while a socially responsible fund is not necessarily inconsistent with ERISA requirements, the managers must first determine that the choice "when judged solely on the basis of its economic value, would be equal to or superior to alternative available investments."

## State Laws on ETIs

Twenty-two pension systems for schoolteachers surveyed by the National Council on Teacher Retirement[12] had explicit statutory authority for ETIs and other activities with a social dimension. Many other public plans participate in ETIs under their general legal authority.[13] The explicit ETI statutes typically authorize, but do not require, ETI investing. Some laws direct fund managers to "consider" ETIs or social goals. The most strongly stated laws are those of Kentucky (giving "priority" to investments benefiting the state economy and requiring the board to solicit proposals from business), Massachusetts (requiring such investments to the extent "reasonably possible"), and Montana ("urging" the board to place up to 3% of funds in locally focused venture capital firms). Notwithstanding these specific directives, all such statutes require continued adherence to the principle of prudence. On the opposite end of the spectrum, Kansas's law prohibits any investment that has economic development or a social purpose as its primary objective. About half of the ETI laws place a quantitative limit on ETI

[10] The DoL bulletin indicates that ETIs could be acceptable for pension plans "although some of these asset categories [such as venture capital] may require a longer time to generate significant investment returns, may be less liquid and may not have as much readily available information..." *Federal Register*, June 23, 1994. p. 32,606.

[11] Labor Department Advisory Opinion 98-04A, in *Pension and Benefits Reporter*, Bureau of National Affairs, Inc. Washington, DC. June 8, 1998. p. 1376-1377.

[12] The survey covered the state pension plans for public school teachers, which in some cases were co-managed with the general state employee plans. The information in this section is derived from the survey as reported in Moore, Cynthia L. *Protecting Retirees' Money.* Austin, TX. National Council on Teacher Retirement. 1995.

[13] For example, California is one of the most prominent in the field even though its law is not explicit on the subject. Under its general authority, California has invested pension funds in mortgages for plan members, housing construction, and venture capital for high technology businesses.

investments, ranging from 1% of plan assets in Arizona to 25% in Florida. The most common statutory limit is 5%.

State ETI laws specify various goals for these investments. Usually the goal is stated in general terms, such as to benefit the state's economy (Arkansas, Colorado, Michigan, Pennsylvania and Rhode Island)[14] or, somewhat more specifically, to stimulate full employment (Iowa and Kentucky). Seven ETI laws are designed to help typed of businesses that are assumed to have restricted access to capital: small business (Michigan), venture capital funds (Montana, Ohio, Texas, Vermont, Wisconsin), in-state commercial banks (Nebraska), and minority- and women-owned firms (Ohio). Other stated goals include housing finance (Connecticut, Florida, Hawaii, Minnesota), public school construction (Tennessee, West Virginia), and local economic development projects (Arizona, Tennessee). At least two states explicitly encourage plans to hire "emerging" investment management firms (Missouri, Wisconsin).

## SPECIFIC INVESTMENT POLICIES OF STATE AND LOCAL PLANS

State pension fund investments for general employee plans usually are controlled by a trustee, a board of trustees, or a similar advisory body with authority to set and approve investment policies. Most states have a board of trustees that oversees the administration of the state retirement plan, including fund investment. These boards vary in size. Only New York has a single state official (the State Comptroller) in charge of fund investment. In some states an advisory board reviews fund investment policies, but in many states the board of trustees sets broad investment policy guidelines within the constraints of state law regarding types of investments. State boards can include elected members, appointed members, and ex-officio members. In the majority of states, board members either are elected directly by plan participants or are appointed to represent plan participants, although about one third of the states do not include members explicitly designated to represent participants. Only two states, South Carolina and West Virginia, have boards composed exclusively of elected state officials. Louisiana is the only state in which all board members are elected by plan participants, although the majority of board members are elected by plan participants in 10 states.

### Legal Lists

In the 19$^{th}$ century, pension trust funds were often required to invest in a "legal list' of safe investments, primarily government bonds and highly rated private bonds. These legal lists, usually set forth in state law, strictly delineated the permitted investments or categories of investments for public plan assets. While some states retain specific requirements for public pension trust funds, most states have adopted the standard of care

---

[14] Rhode Island's law also mentions regional economic development.

that would be exercised by a reasonable person investing his or her own funds. Fourteen states still were using legal lists of some type in 1996; 29% of local plans were subject to legal lists.[15]

Today all state plans can invest in stocks, though some plans are limited by law in regard to the amount of such investment. In 1997, Michigan revamped its pension policies by increasing the amount that state, county, and municipal pension funds can invest in stocks from 60% to 65% of total plan assets, a level that is typical of stock investments by private pension funds.[16] The same law also permits up to 15% of total pension assets to be invested in stock derivatives (e.g., stock market futures) and up to 20% to be invested in foreign securities.[17] Also in 1997, West Virginia, Indiana, and South Carolina, the last three states to prohibit any investment in stocks by their retirement systems, lifted that restriction.[18]

## Corporate Governance

A recent development in the investment behavior of some public funds involves efforts to influence directly the decision-making of corporations in which the funds hold investments. This phenomenon has been made possible by the rapid growth in public fund assets and the fact that corporate equity constitutes a rising share of those assets. With the large holdings of corporate equities by some public funds, these funds potentially have considerable influence on corporate governance. While many plans do not use their stock ownership to influence corporate policies directly, others have tried to use their voting power as shareholders to improve the financial performance of corporations in order to maximize returns to plan participants. This shareholder power also can be used to advance participant and taxpayer interests in regard to the corporate role in environmental improvement, humanitarian concerns, and local economic development. An oft-cited example of this activism was the effort by state employee plans in New York and California to influence the selection of a new board chairman at the General Motors Corporation, a move that these plans' trustees felt would improve the financial outlook of the company and thereby improve the return on investment for the funds.

The California Public Employees' Retirement System (CalPERS), the largest U.C. public pension fund, developed a reputation in the early 1990s as a "shareholder activist," using pension investments as leverage to influence corporate decisions and increase the value of its fund. For example, challenges from CalPERS were thought to have contributed to the dismissal of the chief executives of several corporations that had

[15] Harris, Jennifer D. *From Broad to Specific: The Evolution of Public Pension Investment Restrictions.* Public Retirement Institute, Alexandria, VA. July 1998.

[16] Pension and Investments. *New Michigan Law Opens Asset Classes.* March 3, 1997, p. 33.

[17] A survey of 237 public pension plans found that 24 of the surveyed plans were under legal limits in 1996 regarding foreign investments. The average limit was 8% of assets. Source: Jennifer D. Harris. *Op.cit.*

[18] Bureau of National Affairs, Inc. *PRI Report Examines Restrictions Affecting Public Pension Systems.* v. 24, no. 29. Washington, DC. July 20, 1998, p. 1636.

performed poorly. More recently, some observers have argued that CalPERS' activist reputation may have been overstated and that CalPERS' activism may not have had as great an impact on, or been the most important factor in, the stock market gains of targeted companies.[19]

## Economically Targeted Investments (ETIs)

While private plans, particularly collectively bargained plans, have engaged in ETIs, most ETI activity has occurred in public pension plans. Of the 50 states, 22 had laws that authorized, or directed funding of, ETIs by public pension plans. Other states engage in ETIs under their general authority in accordance with the states' fiduciary prudence standards. A 1995 study by the U.S. General Accounting Office (GAO) found that 29 state plans were involved in ETIs. The GAO report states: "Our list may not be complete, however, given the lack of a nationwide database on ETI activity."[20]

A 1993 study sponsored by the Institute for Fiduciary Education (IFE) and the Ford Foundation, *Economically Targeted Investments*, reported that 42% of the 119 state and local pension plans surveyed were investing in ETIs. Significant sums were invested in ETIs, although the amounts represented only a small fraction of total pension assets. Fifty funds responded that they had invested an aggregate $19.8 billion in such investments. Of this 19.8 billion, housing programs accounted for 64.2%.[21]

A 1996 study of the 20 largest public plans (the *Brancato Report on Institutional Investment*) found that 18 of the 20 had invested $22.7 billion in ETIs in 1995, accounting for 2.9% of their total investments. However, the proportion of assets used for ETIs varied widely among the plans, from 0.5% or less by 7 of the 20 plans to 3.8% by the Wisconsin Investment Board, 5.8% by CalPERS, 6.0% by the California State Teachers Plan, and 8.4% by the New York State & Local Pension Fund.[22]

Large public pension plans and those operating statewide are more likely to have engaged in ETIs than are smaller funds operating in sub-state areas. The 1993 IFE survey reported that relatively few ETI programs were imposed by legislation or external pressure. Most ETIs were advanced by the funds themselves. While boards of trustees of public pension funds were found to have actively promoted ETIs, it should be noted that government officials frequently serve on these boards.

The 1995 GAO study found the performance of ETIs to be similar to that of comparable investments, although performance of ETI venture capital programs sometimes lagged the comparison group of investments. GAO was unable to reach definitive conclusions about the economic effects of ETIs because of inadequate data

---

[19] Institutional Investor. *Low-Cal CalPERS.* March 1997, pp. 41-49.

[20] U.S. General Accounting Office, *Public Pension Plans: Evaluation of Economically Targeted Investment Programs.* GAO/PEMD-95-13. Washington, DC. March 1995.

[21] Bureau of National Affairs, Inc. *BNA Pension and Benefits Reporter.* Washington, DC. June 27, 1994.

[22] Spencer's Research Reports. *Economically Targeted Investments Are Generally Limited to Government and Nonprofit Pension Plans.* Charles D. Spencer & Associates, Inc. Chicago, IL. October 17, 1997. p. 142-1.

from the surveys and studies reviewed. National surveys and studies had too little data on economic effects, and the plans themselves did not collect such data.[23]

Some ETIs were prompted as responses to fiscal emergencies. In the mid-1970s, several New York State and New York City pension funds purchased bonds of the Municipal Assistance Corporation (MAC) to help New York City avoid bankruptcy. To avoid running afoul of the tax law requiring pension funds to be used for the "exclusive benefit" of participants, pension fund trustees asked Congress to enact special legislation to exempt their actions from the rule. Emphasizing the special nature of that situation, not to be interpreted as a precedent for other pension plans in similar circumstances, Congress passed P.L. 94-236 to provide that the purchase of MAC securities would not be considered a violation of the exclusive benefit rule or a prohibited transaction.

In a similar situation, state and local pension funds in Pennsylvania made loans to the City of Philadelphia in the early 1990s to see the city through a temporary cash shortage. Comparable situations have confronted other government entities and their employee pension funds. For example, the City of Detroit used pension funds to bail itself out in the early 1980s. Michigan's Public Employee Pension Fund was asked by the Governor and other state officials to provide a loan to the Chrysler Corporation in the early 1980s.[24] Wisconsin's state pension fund loaned money to the Harley-Davidson Corporation in the 1980s to help that company avoid bankruptcy.[25]

The following discussion provides examples of different approaches that public plans have taken in using plan assets for ETIs.

*Economic Development Projects*

Legislatures across the country have examined the issue of using public pension funds to invest in state economic development. According to a 1990 survey for the National Council of State Legislatures, only 30% of surveyed funds reported having specific permission or encouragement from their legislatures to invest in state economic development projects. Almost half of these plans had no explicit ETI limits. Most of those funds operating under ETI limits had ceilings on economic development projects set between 1% and 8% of total assets.

The portfolios of some of the largest public plans include investments that were made in part to achieve collateral benefits in state economic development. Assets from the Texas Teacher Retirement System and the Permanent University of Texas Fund helped capitalize the Texas Growth Fund, which invests in state economic development projects intended to increase state employment. The Retirement Systems of Alabama invested in the development of that state's Robert Trent Jones Golf Trail to help boost tourism.

One often cited example of economic development by a state pension fund that went awry resulted form a law passed in Kansas in the early 1990 that required 10% of its

[23] U.S. General Accounting Office, *Op.cit.*

[24] Institutional Investor. v. 16, October 1982, p. 173 and p. 175.

[25] BNA Pension Reporter. *Federal Legislation May Be Needed to Protect Plan Investments, Regan Says.* Bureau of National Affairs, Inc. Washington, DC. November 6, 1989. p. 1910.

pension fund to be invested in Kansas businesses. The Kansas ETI program eventually was suspended after several investments in businesses that failed. The Kansas legislature investigated the fund for possible violation of the "prudent investor" rule.[26]

*Housing Investment*

Large pension plans, both public and private, invest in real property and home mortgages. However, public plans are more likely to view these types of investments as a means to stimulate economic development in their own regions or to help provide more affordable housing for area residents. This latter objective sometimes has led to investments in individual home mortgages for a plan's participants. Some states limit the proportion of their plans' assets that can be invested in residential mortgages.

CalPERS invests in a Home Loan Program that provides 100% mortgage financing and funds real estate investment to create housing, jobs, and community development in California. The Pennsylvania State Employees' Retirement System invests in residential and commercial property mortgages, with a requirement that 50% of the commercial real estate investments must be within the state.

Investing in affordable housing for senior citizens is a recent development in public pension real estate investments. The Massachusetts Carpenters' Pension fund and the Retirement Systems of Alabama made decisions to fund such projects, largely to meet perceived social needs in their states, but also in expectation of positive investment yields. With the projected growth of the elderly population, the need for senior housing projects is expected to grow, and such investments provide needed capital for these projects.

*Venture Capital Projects*

Venture capital investments fund the operations of business enterprises that are potentially highly profitable but are at an early state of development and, hence, have an above-average risk of default. Public pension plans invest in venture capital but often set limits on the extent of these investments. According to the NCSL survey, 22 funds indicated that they made venture capital investments, but most plans were limited to investing no more than 5% of their assets in such projects. Among public pension plans, investment in venture capital funds occurs primarily among larger statewide pension plans rather than smaller municipal plans, probably because larger plans are more likely to have the staff and expertise necessary to analyze and track these types of investments.[27]

---

[26] Spencer's Research Reports, *Op.cit.*

[27] American Association of Retired Persons. *Public Employee Pension Funds: Retirement Security for Plan Participants or Cash Cow for State Governments?* Washington, DC. 1993. p. 12.

*Public Infrastructure*

Some state and local governments, faced with an urgent need to repair deteriorating highways and bridges and expand transportation facilities, have viewed pension funds as a way to obtain needed funding for this purpose at reduced borrowing cost. Such investments by public pension funds are seen by advocates as an appropriate use of pension funds, since they hold capital that originated from taxpayer contributions to pension plans. This idea was explored by the Infrastructure Investment Commission, established by act of Congress in 1991, and President Clinton advocated infrastructure investment by pension funds in his 1992 presidential campaign. However, this idea stalled because it faced a major obstacle, namely, the lack of direct financial returns to the pension plan. While general returns to a local economy from infrastructure improvements might profit a pension fund indirectly, direct returns would be needed to justify this use of pension funds in lieu of traditional investment alternatives. Pension funds do not invest in the bond issues often used to finance infrastructure projects because these bonds pay tax-exempt interest and, hence, carry below-market interest rates. The tax break such bonds convey to private investors is of no use to pension funds, public or private, since they already qualify for deferral of tax on investment earnings.

## Social Responsibility Screens

The practice of including or excluding securities from a fund's portfolio based on social criteria first gained attention in the early 1970s. By 1997, the Social Investment Forum's *1997 Report on Responsible Investing Trends in the United States* estimated that $529 billion was invested in socially screened portfolios and mutual funds, compared with only $162 billion as recently as 1995.[28] Of that total, 23% was from public pension funds.

The Social Investment Forum's report found that, of the socially screened public and private portfolios, 84% avoided investing in tobacco companies, 72% screened out companies with gambling interests, and 68% avoided companies that produce alcoholic beverages. Other commonly screened investments were those in firms that manufacture weapons (69%) and that manufacture birth control and/or abortion products (50%). Some social responsibility screening was inclusive rather than exclusive, seeking to invest in companies perceived as pursuing desirable social policies with regard to environmental protection, employee rights, human rights, and animal rights.

A 1996 survey by the Public Pension Coordinating Council found that about 40% of state and local plans that responded to questions about screening used some type of "investment prohibition" in allocating their assets. Some of the screening strategies applied by public pension managers are discussed further below.

---

[28] Spencer's Research Reports. *Socially Responsible Investing Largely Limited to Screened Stock Portfolios.* Charles D. Spencer & Associates, Inc. Chicago, IL. August 7, 1998. p. 142-7.

*Foreign Policy Initiatives*

Public pension plan investment selections have sometimes been made in accordance with the *Sullivan Principles* or the *MacBride Principles*. The Sullivan and MacBride Principles also have been used widely in portfolio screening by private pension plans. The Sullivan Principles were named for a civil rights leader, Leon Sullivan, who led protests against American investment in South Africa. Pension managers were asked to avoid investing in securities of firms doing business in South Africa unless the firms adopted the Sullivan Principles, which called for American companies operating in South Africa to eliminate racial discrimination against non-white South Africans. At one time, 13 states had laws requiring their pension plans to apply the Sullivan Principles in their investment decisions.

The MacBride Principles were developed by an Irish statesman and Nobel Prize winner, Sean MacBride. Pension mangers using this screen avoid investments in American companies doing business in Northern Ireland unless the companies agree to conduct their operations according to the MacBride Principles, which aim to reduce discrimination against Roman Catholic workers in Northern Ireland.[29] In 1994, two states (Connecticut and Massachusetts) required their plans to use the MacBride Principles, and four other states encouraged their use.

Other concerns about foreign investments have led to portfolio screening. In 1994, three states had legal restrictions applicable to investment in specific countries for foreign policy reasons. Recently, student protests about political oppression in Burma led to a 1997 political directive to the Ann Arbor, Michigan municipal plan to divest its portfolio of investments in certain firms doing business with the Burmese government.[30]

*Tobacco Companies*

Some state retirement plans have begun divesting their funds of tobacco stocks. One estimate indicated that state plans sold at least $850 million in shares of tobacco companies in 1996 and 1997. The Maryland State Retirement System was the first fund to sell all of its tobacco stocks, which were worth $75 million in April 1996. The largest state plan divestment of tobacco stocks occurred in June 1997 when the Florida State Board of Administration sold shares worth $650 million.[31]

Public pension plans may find it difficult to eliminate tobacco stocks from their portfolios completely, because most tobacco companies have diversified into other

---

[29] The *MacBride Principles* call for increased representation of "underrepresented religious groups" in the workforce, security of travel, a ban on provocative religious demonstrations in the workplace, equal employment opportunities, efforts to recruit and train minority group employees, and appointment of an affirmative action officer from the ranks of senior management.

[30] Fulman, Ricki. *Investors Push to Cut Myanmar Ties*. Pensions & Investments. New York, NY. November 10, 1997.

[31] Narayan, Shoba. *The Smokeless Portfolio*. Institutional Investor. New York, NY. September 1997. p. 187.

industries, and their stocks have continued to appreciate in value. Public pension investment officers, in light of their fiduciary responsibility to maximize plan returns for a given level of risk, may find complete divestment unwise in the short run. However, some financial analysts have voiced concern about the long-term financial health of tobacco stocks because of pending multibillion-dollar class-action lawsuits. Still, some observers argue that the pressure on plan managers to divest is more political than financial.

Despite the widespread view that the use of tobacco products should be discouraged, some states have been reluctant to divest their tobacco stocks because of good returns. In 1997, public pension systems with the largest tobacco holdings were those in New York ($583 million), Texas ($477 million), Ohio ($475 million), and New Jersey ($420 million).[32]

*Environmental Concerns*

Interest in environmental screening of portfolios grew after the *Exxon Valdez* oil spill in Alaskan waters in 1989. That environmental disaster led to development of the *Valdez Principles*, which later became known as the *CERES Principles*.[33] These principles can be used by plans to identify companies that violate CERES standards for desirable corporate behavior toward the environment. The securities of those companies can be avoided in investment choices made by plan managers. CalPERS was one of the first public pension plans to endorse the use of these principles.

*Social Mores and the Entertainment Industry*

In 1998, the Texas State Employee Retirement Association considered a social responsibility screen to remove a single company's stock from its portfolio. In this case, pension plan members raised a concern that the Walt Disney Corporation has produced films that were too sexually explicit for the target audience and, hence, were in violation of the mores of the plan's membership. However, legislation necessary to implement this screen did not receive final approval.

*Emerging Issues*

Other high visibility issues may emerge as focal points for social responsibility screening by plan managers. These emerging issues include gun control (targeting gun manufacturers and retailers), and animal rights (targeting firms that violate standards for the treatment of animals).

---

[32] Spencer's Research Reports, *Op.cit.*

[33] CERES is an abbreviation for the Coalition for Environmentally Responsible Economies, a consortium of investment professionals and organizations interested in promoting socially responsible investing.

## Non-Financial Factors in the Hiring of Investment Managers

In 1994, five states had laws that encouraged affirmative action by public pension plans in their hiring of investment managers. However, in California, where public plans hold about $165 billion in assets, a recent anti-affirmative action initiative passed by voters may redirect away from minority-owned and women-owned firms some of the $150 million in fees that are paid by California pension funds to money managers, brokerages, consultants, and other business service providers. That initiative, Proposition 209, prohibits all California state or local governments from preferential treatment by race or gender in regard to public employment, contracting, and education. Some large California pension plans, including the Los Angeles Fire and Police Retirement System, the Los Angeles County Employees Retirement Association, and the San Diego City Employees Retirement System, have programs that direct a portion of their securities trading to women- and minority-owned investment management firms but do not set quotas or designate proportions of contracts for such allocations. These plans believe that their programs will not be affected by the new law. Other pension systems are concerned that the composition of their in-house pension staff could be affected as well as their contracts with investment managers.

Other non-financial factors sometimes affect the hiring of investment managers. Public pension plans often hire regional firms rather than national firms to support local or regional employment. Plans also have hired investment managers on the basis of political support. This latter practice of requiring investment advisors to make political contributions, either implicitly or explicitly, in order to gain investment management contracts has become known as the "pay to play" problem. This practice is under scrutiny by the Securities and Exchange Commission (SEC). The SEC may propose a rule to address this practice in the agency's role as regulator of the practices of investment advisers.[34]

[34] BNA Pension Reporter. *Public Pension 'Pay-to-Play' Rule Possible in April or May, Levitt Says.* Bureau of National Affairs, Inc. Washington, DC. April 5, 1999. p. 998.

# LEGAL ISSUES AFFECTING THE RIGHT OF STATE EMPLOYEES TO BRING SUIT UNDER THE AGE DISCRIMINATION IN EMPLOYMENT ACT AND OTHER FEDERAL LABOR LAWS

*Kimberly D. Jones*

On January 11, 2000, the United States Supreme Court held in *Kimel v. Florida Board of Regents* that state employees could not bring suit against a state under the Age Discrimination in Employment Act (ADEA) because of sovereign immunity.[1] The ADEA prohibits discrimination in employment based on age.[2] Under the 11th Amendment of the U.S. Constitution, states are immune from suit unless the state consents or an exception applies. This is not the first time the Court has addressed the scope of state's rights. The *Kimel* case reflects a growing jurisprudence governing the interaction between the federal government and states. This issue has a direct impact on Congress' ability to enact legislation, particularly labor laws, that apply to state employees. This report discusses the cases that have preceded *Kimel* and then provides a discussion of the *Kimel* decision.

## 11TH AMENDMENT AND RECENT U.S. SUPREME COURT DECISIONS

The Eleventh Amendment of the U.S. Constitution states that:

---

[1] 139 F.3d 1426 (11th Cir. 1998), *reh'g denied*, 157 F.3d908 (11th Cir. 1998), *cert. granted*, 67 U.S.L.W. 3464 (U.S. Jan. 25, 1999)(No. 98-791)(No. 98-796), *aff'd*, No. 98-791, No. 98-796, slip op. (U.S. Jan. 11, 2000)

[2] For a detailed discussion of the Age Discrimination in Employment Act, see CRS Report 97-479, *The Age Discrimination in Employment Act (ADEA): Overview and Current Legal Developments*, by Kimberly D. Jones.

> The Judicial power of the United States shall not be construed to extend to any suit in law or equity, commenced or prosecuted against on of the United States by Citizens of another State, or by citizens or Subjects of any Foreign State.[3]

The U.S. Supreme Court has interpreted this constitutional provision in a number of decisions. A long history precedes the present series of cases.[4] The most significant of recent cases includes *Seminole Tribe of Florida v. Florida* in which the Court held that the "Eleventh Amendment prevents congressional authorization of suits by private parties against unconsenting States."[5] The Court used a two-part test to determine whether Congress had properly "abrogated the State's immunity from suit."[6] The first part of the test was whether Congress explicitly expressed its intent to unilaterally abrogate state immunity, and the second was whether Congress had exercised proper authority in doing so. According to the *Seminole Tribe* Court, "Congress' intent to abrogate the States' immunity from suit must be obvious from a 'clear legislative statement.'"[7] The Court stated that authorizing suit in federal court is not enough to show Congress intended to abrogate state immunity.[8] Further, the Court noted that "mere receipt of federal funds cannot establish that a State has consented to suit in federal court."[9] After finding express intent to abrogate state immunity in the text of the statute in question, the Court turned its attention to whether Congress had exercised valid authority. Chief Justice Rehnquist, writing for the majority, "held that through the Fourteenth Amendment, federal power extended to intrude upon the province of the Eleventh Amendment and therefore that § 5 of the Fourteenth Amendment allowed Congress to abrogate the immunity from suit guaranteed by that Amendment."[10] Section 5 of the Fourteenth Amendment gives Congress the power to enforce the provisions of the Fourteenth Amendment.[11] However, the statute in question was enacted pursuant to Congress' power under the Indian Commerce Clause of the Constitution.[12] The Court held that neither the Indian Commerce Clause nor the Interstate Commerce Clause provided Congress authority to abrogate a state's sovereign immunity under the 11th Amendment.[13]

In its most recent term, the Court revisited the scope of the 11th Amendment in a series of cases. In *Alden v. Maine*, a group of state employees filed suit against the state

---

[3] U.S. Const. amend. XI.

[4] For a detailed discussion of the evolution of the 11th Amendment, see CRS Report RL30315, *Federalism and the Constitution: Limits on Congressional Power*, by Kenneth R. Thomas (Sept. 21, 1999).

[5] 517 U.S. 44, 72 (1996). According to the Court, "The Eleventh Amendment prohibits Congress from making the State of Florida capable of being sued in federal court." Id. at 76.

[6] 517 U.S. at 55.

[7] 517 U.S. at 55 (quoting Green v. Mansour, 474 U.S. 64, 68 (1985)).

[8] 517 U.S. at 56.

[9] 517 U.S. at 59 (quoting Atascadero State Hospital v. Scanlon, 473 U.S. 234, 238-239 (1985)).

[10] 517 U.S. at 59. *See* Fitzpatrick v. Bitzer, 427 U.S. 445, 452-456 (1976).

[11] Section 1of the Fourteenth Amendment states in part that: "No State shall make or enforce any law which shall abridge the privileges or immunities of citizens of the United States; nor shall any State deprive any person of life, liberty, or property, without due process of law; nor deny to any person within its jurisdiction the equal protection of the laws." U.S. Const. amend. XIV, § 1.

[12] U.S. Const. art. 1, § 8, cl. 3.

[13] 517 U.S. at 72-73.

to recover under the Fair Labor Standards Act (FLSA).[14] The federal district court dismissed the action based on the Court's decision in *Seminole Tribe*. The employees re-filed the case in state court which also dismissed the case on grounds of sovereign immunity. However, the Maine Supreme Court's decision conflicted with a decision by the Arkansas Supreme Court. The U.S. Supreme Court took the appeal to decide whether such claims could proceed in state court, even though the 11$^{th}$ Amendment applies only to federal courts. Ultimately, the Court held that "the powers delegated to Congress under Article I [Interstate Commerce Clause] of the United States Constitution do not include the power to subject non-consenting States to private suits for damages in state courts."[15]

In conclusion, the Court noted that states can be sued under limited circumstances: states may be sued if they consent;[16] the United States may bring suit against a state; and a state may be sued to enforce legislation enacted pursuant to § 5 of the Fourteenth Amendment. The Court also noted that the 11$^{th}$ Amendment only concerns suits against states, but it did not "extend to suits prosecuted against a municipal corporation or other governmental entity which is not an arm of the State."[17] Nor does the 11$^{th}$ Amendment "bar all suits against state officers."[18] The Court stated:

> The rule, however, does not bar certain actions against state officers for injunctive or declaratory relief...Even a suit for money damages may be prosecuted against a state officer in his individual capacity for unconstitutional or wrongful conduct fairly attributable to the officer himself, so long as the relief is sought not from the state treasury but from the officer personally.[19]

The rule established under *Ex Parte Young* allows an individual to bring suit for prospective or injunctive relief against a state officer to prevent the officer from continued violations of the statute.[20] Such an injunction preventing future violation by a state official could be enforced in federal or state court and would effectively prevent the state, through its officers, from continuing to violate federal law.

---

[14] 527 U.S. ____, No. 98-436 (U.S. June 23, 1999).

[15] No. 98-436, slip op. at 2.

[16] The Court has made it clear in numerous decisions that a "State's consent to suit must be 'unequivocally expressed.'" No. 98-149, slip op. at 8 (quoting *Pennhurst State School and Hospital v. Halderman*, 465 U.S. 89, 99 (1984). *See also* Atascadero State Hospital v. Scanlon, 473 U.S. 234, 241 (1985). See also *College Savings Bank v. Florida Prepaid Postsecondary Education Expense Board*, 527 U.S.____, No. 98-149 (U.S. June 23) (rejecting argument that Florida voluntarily or impliedly waived its sovereign immunity by participating in interstate commerce activities regulated by federal law.) In *Seminole Tribe*, the Court stated that "mere receipt of federal funds cannot establish that a State has consented to suit in federal court." 517 U.S. at 59 (quoting Atascadero State Hospital v. Scanlon, 473 U.S. 234, 238-239 (1985). Consent may be shown where "the State voluntarily invokes [federal court] jurisdiction or else if the State makes a 'clear declaration' that it intends to submit itself to [federal court] jurisdiction." No. 98-149, slip op. at 8 (citations omitted).

[17] No. 98-436, slip op. at 47.

[18] No. 98-436, slip op. at 48. *See* Ex Parte Young, 209 U.S. 123 (1908).

[19] No. 98-436, slip op. at 48.

[20] 209 U.S. 123 (1908).

In *Alden*, the Court noted that the federal government retains the right to sue a state to enforce federal law. A logical extension of this could be the United States bringing suit under federal law against a state on behalf of affected citizens. But, it is not completely clear whether the government could do so. The issue may be addressed by the Court in its current term when it will decide whether the United States can authorize citizens to sue states in the name of the United States.[21]

## SUIT UNDER SECTION 5 OF THE FOURTEENTH AMENDMENT

A state's sovereign immunity may be abrogated if an individual is suing under a federal law that was enacted pursuant to Congress' power under Section 5 of the Fourteenth Amendment. Section 1 of the Fourteenth Amendment states in part that, "No State shall make or enforce any law which shall abridge the privileges or immunities of citizens of the United States; nor shall any State deprive any person of life, liberty, or property, without due process of law; nor deny to any person within its jurisdiction the equal protection of the laws."[22] Section 5 of the Fourteenth Amendment states that, "The Congress shall have power to enforce, by appropriate legislation, the provisions of this article."[23]

In *City of Boerne v. Flores*, the Court struck down the Religious Freedom Restoration Act (RFRA) on the grounds that the enactment of RFRA exceeded Congress' power.[24] RFRA provided that the government could not burden a person's exercise of religion, even by a generally applicable law, unless the government showed that the burden "(1) is in furtherance of a compelling governmental interest; and (2) is the least restrictive means of furthering that compelling governmental interest."[25] RFRA applied to any federal, state, or local government statute, ordinance or regulation. RFRA was enacted in response to the Court's decision in *Employment Div., Dept. of Human Resources of Oregon v. Smith*,[26] which "held that neutral, generally applicable laws may be applied to religious practices even when not supported by a compelling governmental interest."[27]

---

[21] *See* Vermont Agency of Natural Resources v. United States ex rel. Stevens, 162 F.3d 195 (2nd Cir. 1998), *cert. granted*, 67 U.S.L.W. 3717 (U.S. Jun. 24, 1999)(No. 98-1828). This case was brought under the False Claims Act which imposes liability on a person for filing a false monetary claim with the United States government. FCA allows an individual to bring suit under the act in the name of the United States. The United States is notified of the action and given the opportunity to intervene or to dismiss the suit. The action remains in the name of the United States, but an individual that is allowed to proceed may recover a portion of the recovery; the remainder goes to the United States. The lower court held that such suits were not a violation of the 11th Amendment because the 11th Amendment does not prevent suits against states by the U.S.

[22] U.S. Const. amend. XIV, § 1.

[23] U.S. Const. amend. XIV, § 5.

[24] 521 U.S. 507 (1997).

[25] Id. at 516.

[26] 494 U.S. 872 (1990).

[27] 521 U.S. at 514.

The issue before the Court was whether RFRA was "a proper exercise of Congress' § 5 power 'to enforce' by 'appropriate legislation' the constitutional guarantee that no State shall deprive any person of life, liberty, or property, without due process of law," nor deny any person 'equal protection of the laws.'"[28] The Court looked to the history of Section 5 and found that it granted Congress the power to enact legislation that would enforce Section 5, but not the power to create new rights under Section 5.[29] RFRA did not apply merely to laws targeting religious discrimination or bigotry, but to any law that had the effect of burdening the free exercise of religion. The Court found that the legislative history did not reflect a recent history of religious persecution or a "widespread pattern of religious discrimination in this country."[30] Aside from the legislative history, the Court found that RFRA's sweeping application was "so out of proportion to a supposed remedial or preventive object that it cannot be understood as responsive to, or designed to prevent, unconstitutional behavior."[31] RFRA, according to the Court, was not remedial legislation to enforce an existing constitutional right, but instead created a new right and therefore was beyond Congress' power to enact.[32]

In *Florida Prepaid Postsecondary Ed. Expense Bd. v. College Savings Bank*, the Court again addressed the scope of Congress' authority under Section 5 of the Fourteenth Amendment.[33] Reiterating the holding in *Boerne*, the Court noted that the term "enforce" used in Section 5 should be taken seriously. Section 5 should not be used to create a new federal right, but only to enforce a right under the 14th Amendment. The Court stated, "We thus hold that for Congress to invoke § 5, it must identify conduct transgressing the Fourteenth Amendment's substantive provisions, and must tailor its legislative scheme to remedying or preventing such conduct."[34]

To summarize, the Court's recent cases hold that Congress may not authorize an individual to bring suit against a state in federal or state court to enforce a federal statute without: (1) the state's consent or (2) express Congressional abrogation of state sovereign immunity subject to legislation enacted pursuant to an appropriate exercise of jurisdiction under § 5 of the Fourteenth Amendment. The Court's cases note that the 11th Amendment does not bar suit against a state by the federal government. The issue of whether an individual may bring suit against a state in the name of the federal government will be decided during the Court's current term. The Court has also held that the 11th Amendment does not bar suits against state officers for injunctive or declaratory relief or even damages if the damages are sought individually from the state officer. The Eleventh Amendment does not apply to municipal corporations or other governmental entities, i.e., a city or county government.

---

28 521 U.S. at 517.

29 The Court in *Boerne* state, "Congress does not enforce a constitutional right by changing what the right is. It has been given the power 'to enforce,' not the power to determine what constitutes a constitutional violation." Id. at 519.

30 Id. at 531.

31 Id. at 532.

32 Id. at 532-534.

33 527 U.S.____, No. 98-531 (U.S. June 23, 1999).

34 Id.

# *KIMEL V. FLORIDA BOARD OF REGENTS*

In *Kimel v. Florida Board of Regents*, plaintiffs in two separate ADEA cases appealed to the U.S. Supreme Court for a review of the 11th Circuit's holding that the state was not subject to suit under the ADEA because of sovereign immunity.[35] The Court considered whether: (1) the ADEA contains a clear abrogation of states' immunity and (2) whether Congress' extension of the ADEA to states was a proper exercise of Congress' power under Section 5 of the 14th Amendment to abrogate immunity.[36] Ultimately, the U.S. Supreme Court held that Congress did give notice of its intent to abrogate state immunity, but lacked the constitutional authority under Section 5 of the 14th Amendment to do so.[37]

According to the Court, the issue boiled down to two questions: "first, whether Congress unequivocally expressed its intent to abrogate [a state's sovereign immunity]; and second, if it did, whether Congress acted pursuant to a valid grant of constitutional authority."[38] At to the first question, the Court found that congress' amendments to the ADEA that expanded the definition of employer to include states and that incorporated provisions of the Fair Labor Standards Act (FLSA), which authorized suits in any Federal or State court of competent jurisdiction, "clearly demonstrates Congress' intent to subject the States to suit...at the hands of individual employees."[39] The Court rejected the argument that Congress was in any way unclear about its intention to subject states to suit under the ADEA.

Turning to the second question, the Court reiterated its holding from *Seminole Tribe* and later cases, that "Congress lacks power under Article I to abrogate the States' sovereign immunity."[40] The majority opinion states that authority to abrogate does exist under Section 5 of the Fourteenth Amendment.[41] However, this authority is limited. According to the majority, Congress "has been given the power 'to enforce,' not the

---

[35] 139 F.3d 1426 (11th Cir. 1998) *reh'g denied*, 157 F.3d 908 (11th Cir. 1998), *cert. granted*, 67 U.S.L.W. 3464 (U.S. Jan. 26, 1999) (No. 98-796) (No. 98-791). The district court opinions in two of the cases, Kimel v. Florida Board of Regents and Dickson v. Florida Department of Corrections, are unreported. The district court opinion in MacPherson v. University of Montevallo is reported at 938 F. Supp. 785 (N.D. Ala. 1996). The three-judge panel that heard the appeal for the 11th Circuit issued a split decision. Judge Edmondson, writing the decision for the court, held that the ADEA expressly abrogated state immunity but that Congress did not have authority under Section 5 to do so, and therefore there was no abrogation. This decision was joined by Judge Cox, but Chief Judge Hatchett dissented finding both a congressional intent to abrogate and congressional authority under Section 5.

[36] 67 U.S.L.W. 3464 (U.S. Jan. 26, 1999) (No. 98-791) (No. 98-796).

[37] No. 98-791, slip op. at 2. Chief Justice Rehnquist and Justices Scalia, Kennedy, and Thomas joined in parts I, II, and IV of the decision. Part III was joined by Chief Justice Rehnquist and Justices Stevens, Scalia, Souter, Ginsburg, and Breyer. Justice Stevens wrote separately, dissenting in part and concurring in part, which was joined by Justices Souter, Ginsburg, and Breyer. Justice Thomas wrote an opinion concurring and dissenting in part joined by Justice Kennedy.

[38] No. 98-791, slip op. at 8.

[39] No. 98-791, slip op. at 9.

[40] No. 98-791, slip op. at 14.

[41] Id. at 15.

power to determine *what constitutes* a constitutional violation."[42] Noting that it is a difficult line that Congress must follow, the Court "held that '[t]here must be a congruence and proportionality between the injury to be prevented or remedied and the means adopted to that end.'"[43]

Applying the congruence and proportionality test in this instance, the Court found that the ADEA was a disproportionate response "to any unconstitutional conduct that conceivably could be targeted by the Act."[44] The Court noted that in three previous cases, it had "held that the age classifications at issue did not violate the Equal Protection Clause."[45] Moreover, the Court stated that age classifications may be tailored to meet a legitimate state interest, particularly since age, unlike race or sex, is not a suspect classification.[46] It fails to be a suspect classification because older people "have not been subjected to a 'history of purposeful unequal treatment' and old age...does not define a discrete and insular minority..."[47] Finally, the majority opinion concluded that "the ADEA is: 'so out of proportion to a supposed remedial or preventive object that it cannot be understood as responsive to, or designed to prevent, unconstitutional behavior.'"[48] The original plaintiffs argued that the ADEA was enacted to eliminate arbitrary age discrimination which would likely violate the Equal Protection Clause. The Court disagreed, finding "that the ADEA's protection extends beyond the requirements of the Equal Protection Clause."[49]

The Court observed that although the behavior targeted by the ADEA is unlikely to be unconstitutional, the analysis does not end there. Congress may enact prophylactic legislation. The Court then questioned whether the ADEA is a form of "enforcement" or an attempt by Congress to redefine the substance of Section 5. After reviewing the ADEA's legislative history and finding a dearth of a pattern or history of age discrimination, the Court concluded that "Congress' 1974 extension of the Act to the States was an unwarranted response to a perhaps inconsequential problem."[50]

Ultimately, the Court stated, "[We] hold that the ADEA is not a valid exercise of Congress' power under § 5 of the Fourteenth Amendment. The ADEA's purported abrogation of the States' sovereign immunity is accordingly invalid."[51] However, the Court pointed out that state employees are still able to seek recourse under state age discrimination laws.[52]

Justice Stevens wrote a separate opinion, dissenting and concurring in part, joined by Justices Souter, Ginsburg and Breyer. He took issue with the "judge-made doctrine of

[42] Id. at 17. (Emphasis in text).
[43] Id. (quoting City of Boerne v. Flores, 521 U.S. 507, 520 (1998)).
[44] Id. at 18.
[45] Id.
[46] Id. at 19.
[47] Id. at 19.
[48] Id. at 22 (quoting City of Boerne v. Flores, 521 U.S. 507, 532).
[49] Id. at 24.
[50] Id. at 25. Justice O'Connor noted, "Congress never identified any pattern of age discrimination by the States, much less any discrimination whatsoever that rose to the level of constitutional violation." Id.
[51] Id. at 27.
[52] Id. at 25.

sovereign immunity" and argued that if Congress has the authority to enact legislation that is applicable to the states, it also has the authority to determine who may bring enforcement proceedings.[53]

Justice Thomas dissented from the part of the Court's decision that found clear congressional intent to abrogate under the ADEA.[54] He argued that it is not clear that Congress understood or was aware that the changes it made to abrogate state immunity under FLSA would also apply to the ADEA because of the ADEA's incorporation of the enforcement provisions of FLSA.[55] Justice Thomas concurred with the remaining parts of the decision that Congress did not have authority under Section 5 of the 14th Amendment to abrogate state immunity under the ADEA.

## IMPACT OF THE *KIMEL* DECISION

The impact of the *Kimel* decision is still being debated. While state employees may continue to bring suit under state law, *Kimel* does foreclose an avenue of enforcement that had been available to approximately 5 million employees since 1974. It also effectively eliminates the ability of state employees to bring suit under other federal labor laws in which the state has not consented or where Congress does not have § 5 authority. In a larger sense, *Kimel* and *Alden* shift to the federal government a greater role in ensuring state compliance with federal labor law. The *Kimel* decision implies that only suspect classifications such as race or gender would likely meet the "congruence and proportionality" test. However, that proposition as it applies to gender has been put into question after the Court requested that lower courts reevaluate the application of the Equal Pay Act, a federal statute that prohibits gender-based wage discrimination, to states.[56]

---

[53] No. 98-791, slip op. at 5 (Stevens, J., concurring in part, dissenting in part). Justice Stevens stated, "There is not a word in the text of the Constitution supporting the Court's conclusion that the judge-made doctrine of sovereign immunity limits Congress' power to authorize private parties, as well as federal agencies, to enforce federal law against the States." Id.

[54] No. 98-791, slip op. at 3 (Thomas, J., concurring in part, dissenting in part). Justice Thomas referred to the Court's decision in Employees of Dept. of Public Health & Welfare of Mo. v. Department of Public Health & Welfare of Mo., 411 U.S. 279, 285 (1973). He noted that, "In *Employees*, we confronted the pre-1974 version of the [FLSA and]...held that this language fell short of a clear statement of Congress' intent to abrogate." Id. at 3.

[55] Justice Thomas wrote: This sequence of events suggests, in my view, that we should approach with circumspection any theory of 'clear statement by incorporation.' Where Congress amends an Act whose provisions are incorporated by other Acts, the bill under consideration does not necessarily mention the incorporating references in those other Acts, and so fails to inspire confidence that Congress has deliberated on the consequences of the amendment for the other Acts. That is the case here. The legislation that amended [the FSLA]...did not even acknowledge [the enforcement provision of the ADEA]. And, given the purpose of the clear statement rule to 'assur[e] that the legislature has in fact faced' the issue of abrogation,...I am unwilling to indulge the fiction that Congress, when it amended [FLSA], recognized the consequences for a separate Act (the ADEA) that incorporates the amended provision. Id. at 5.

[56] 29 U.S.C.A. § 206(d) (West Supp. 1999).

The Court has ordered two lower courts to reconsider, in light of its decision in *Kimel*, their decisions to allow an Equal Pay Act claim to proceed against two state universities.[57] It is not clear if this issue will reach the Court. Also, on January 21, 2000, the Court agreed to hear *Dickson v. Florida Department of Corrections* to determine if the 11th Amendment prohibits state employees from bringing suit under the Americans with Disabilities Act (ADA).[58] In *Kimel*, a three-judge panel of the 11th Circuit Court of Appeals heard a consolidated appeal of three cases regarding 11th Amendment immunity. Two of the cases dealt with the ADEA and that issue was addressed by the U.S. Supreme Court in *Kimel*. The remaining case, *Dickson*, dealt with the ADA. The lower court panel was split with two of the judges finding abrogation of sovereign immunity under the ADA.

In light of the Court's recent decisions, state employees are unable to bring suit under the Fair Labor Standards Act and the Age Discrimination in Employment Act. However, these statutes may be enforced by administrative action. State employees may also have recourse under an applicable state law. Whether state employees can bring suit under the Equal Pay Act or the Americans with Disabilities Act is a question that the Court is likely to address in the near future.

---

[57] Varner v. Illinois State University, 150 F.3d 706 (7th Cir. 1998), *cert. granted and judgment vacated and remanded*, 67 U.S.L.W. 3469 (Jan. 18, 2000) (No. 98-1117); Anderson v. State University of New York at New Paltz, 169 F.3d 117 (2nd Cir. 1999), *cert. granted and judgment remanded*, 2000 WL 29247 (Jan. 18, 2000) (No. 98-1845). The Equal Pay Act prohibits wage discrimination based on sex. 29 U.S.C.A. § 206 (West Supp. 1999). See also Timmer v. Michigan Department of Commerce, 104 F.3d 833 (6th Cir. 1997)(holding that Equal Pay Act abrogated state's immunity pursuant to valid Congressional power); O'Sullivan v. Minnesota, 191 F.3d 965 (8th Cir. 1999)(holding that Congress properly abrogated state's immunity under the Equal Pay Act).

[58] 139 F.3d 1426 (11th Cir. 1998), *reh'g denied*, 157 F.3d 908 (11th Cir. 1998), *cert. granted*, 2000 WL46077 (U.S. Jan. 21, 2000) (No. 98-829). The district court opinion in Dickson v. Florida Department of Corrections is unreported. For a detailed discussion of the 11th Amendment and the ADA see CRS Report RS20472, *The Americans with Disabilities Act: Eleventh Amendment Issues*, by Nancy Jones (February 16, 2000).

# The Federal Money Trail: Data Sources on Federal Aid, Grants, Loans and Procurement in States and Local Areas

*James R. Riehl*

In times of fiscal restraint, more public and media attention is paid to how much and where the federal government is spending its money. Economists, government officials, researchers, and the public need accurate statistics to determine the location of federal spending, shifts in federal spending, or the impact of federal spending on the economy and on the disparate regional, state, and local economies.

Obtaining statistics concerning the geographic distribution of federal funds through domestic assistance programs, federal procurement activity, loans, and other means, however, can be a frustrating pursuit. No single source has been published that has consistently reported the distribution of federal funds by State, county, city, congressional district, program, and agency. Various reports have been published over the years, but any publication that has been available has had its limitations or has been discontinued. The resources described in this report can aid interested persons in obtaining statistics relating to various aspects of the geographic distribution of federal funds, federal procurement activity, and federal domestic assistance programs.

Care must be taken, however, when attempting to compare figures from the different sources. One must pay strict attention to the introduction and explanatory notes in each document. Each publication's notes will explain what is included and what is excluded; whether the figures are actual expenditures or obligations; whether figures for congressional districts are available; and other important distinctions. This report presents a listing and overview of the various publications that have been issued by the federal government showing the geographic distribution of federal funds.

# FEDERAL AID TO STATES AND LOCAL AREAS

## Federal Expenditures by State
## Consolidated Federal Funds Report

*Federal Expenditures by State (FES)* and the *Consolidated Federal Funds Report (CFFR)* are the government's current publications showing the geographic distribution of federal funds. They are published within 180 days of the close of each fiscal year (September 30) and are usually published in March by the Department of Commerce, Bureau of the Census. Categories of spending included in these reports are: grants, salaries and wages, procurement, loans, insurance, direct payments to individuals, and other direct payments.

*FES* and the *CFFR* were originally published under authority of the Consolidated Federal Funds Report Amendments of 1985 (P.L. 99-547).

*Federal Expenditures by State* was first published in February 1983. At that time, *Federal Expenditures by State for Fiscal Year 1981* and *Federal Expenditures by State for Fiscal year 1982* were both published, retrospectively. Each year since then a volume has been published. The latest report available is for fiscal year 1995. This report contains statistics on federal expenditures to the state level only.

The *Consolidated Federal Funds Report* was published as a two-volume set for fiscal years 1983 through 1993. Volume I was for county areas and Volume II was for sub-county areas. No county or sub-county statistics are available for either fiscal year 1981 or fiscal year 1982. Beginning with fiscal year 1994, the Bureau of the Census ceased publication of the hard copy version of Volume II of the *CFFR* for sub-county areas. Statistics from the fiscal year 1994 sub-county volume are *only* available on a 31/2-inch computer disk. The statistics are in several zipped (compressed) files on the disk, along with an unzip program, zipped Windows and DOS software for viewing/printing the files, and uncompressed files containing explanatory text. *CFFR* Volume I for county areas is also included on the disk, in addition to being available in hard copy. No disk or hard copy version of *CFFR* Volume II for sub-county areas was published for fiscal year 1995. The latest *CFFR* volume available for county areas is for fiscal year 1995.

*Federal Expenditures by State* and the *Consolidated Federal Funds Report* differ somewhat. Figures presented in *Federal Expenditures by State* are actual expenditures while figures in the *CFFR* generally represent obligations but may also include expenditures, depending upon the category in question. Essentially, expenditures are actual payments of monies and obligations are commitments requiring payment in a current or future period. Consult the explanatory notes in each volume for additional information on inclusions, exclusions, and distinctions.

Also note that the initial recipient of monies under various federal programs is a state government. Monies received for certain of these programs may eventually be distributed to local government or other entities within the state, but the monies received are generally recorded in the *CFFR* at the county in which the state capital is located. Block grants, for example, provide federal monies to the states for specific uses. The states are responsible for the final distribution of the monies and are not required to provide the federal government with a detailed accounting of how each dollar was distributed within the state. To obtain data on the distribution of this type of federal monies within a state, one must contact state officials.

Congressional districts are indicated in both volumes of the CFFR set. However, statistics for any county having two or more congressional districts within its borders are not further divided. Listings for counties having more than one district show only the congressional district numbers existing in that county. Making accurate estimates of the distribution of federal funds to congressional districts is an extremely difficult task. If a Member's district is constructed solely along county lines, some estimates of federal monies arriving in that district can be made. However, in many cases, county boundaries do not coincide with congressional district lines. In certain instances, cities located within a county are not actually part of the county for governmental purposes but are independent cities. Parts of a single county can be in several congressional districts. Many congressional districts are so irregularly shaped, containing (parts of) several ZIP codes, it is difficult to ascertain precisely in which congressional district a recipient of federal monies is located. This problem is especially acute in urban areas. Also, as stated earlier in this report, the location where the federal money is initially received is not necessarily where the money actually is spent. This occurs not only for certain grant programs but also for procurement activities. For example, XYZZ Corporation might be awarded a $10 million federal contract to supply widgets to the federal government. The money is initially recorded as received at XYZZ's corporate headquarters in King of Prussia, PA. XYZZ then builds the widgets (and spends much of the money) at its manufacturing facilities in town (and congressional districts) in South Carolina and New York.

Copies of *Federal Expenditures by State* and the *CFFR* are distributed to regional depository libraries and to selected congressional and governmental offices. Copies are available to the public for use at the depository libraries or from the U.S. Government Printing Office for a fee.

Superintendent of Documents
U.S. Government Printing Office
Washington, DC 20402
202/512-1800

The Bureau of the Census has also released CD-ROM versions of the CFFR. Each covers a 10-year period. The CD-ROMs are for 1983-1992, 1984-1993, and 1985-1994. The 1986-1995 edition is scheduled for release in August 1996. Copies are distributed to federal depository libraries. They are available for a fee from Census.

Customer Service
Bureau of the Census
Washington, DC 20233
301/457-4100

The *CFFR* county areas volumes for fiscal year 1994 and 1995 are available at the Bureau of the Census Home Page on the World Wide Web (http://www.census.gov). One may go directly to the *CFFR* section of the Census site (http://www.census.gov/pub/govs/www/cffr.html) if necessary. Statistics for each state or territory may be viewed individually for each fiscal year. It is not necessary to download the entire document to view one state or territory's statistics.

As of July 1996, the *Federal Expenditures by State* volumes are **not** available via the Census Web site due to complications with data transfer to the Internet. The Bureau of the Census is working on the problem with *FES* data transfer and plans to make the *FES* figures available on its Web site at a later date.

States and territories often publish their own materials detailing the geographic distribution of federal and state monies within their borders. If one is attempting to collect as much data as possible concerning the flow of federal funds within a particular state, it is advisable to contact the state for information on publications that contain such data. Contact a state's budget office, the governor's office, or the state library system for assistance with locating relevant materials.

## Federal Outlays
## Geographic Distribution of Federal Funds

In fiscal year 1969 the Office of Economic Opportunity (OEO) began publication of *Federal Outlays (FO). Federal Outlays* was a 53-volume set, with one volume for each state, one for the District of Columbia, one for the territories and other areas, and one summary volume for the entire country. FO was the first government publication that reported distribution of federal funds at the sub-state level. Each volume contained detailed charts shoeing: federal dollars going to the state by department or agency, overall state figures, county statistics, and figures for each city exceeding 25,000 in population. *Catalog of Federal Domestic Assistance (CFDA)* program numbers were also indicated. Congressional districts were not. Single state reports were distributed to Members of Congress, various state and county officials, and depository libraries. Complete sets were sent to the White House, various congressional committees, major federal agencies, and to select public interest groups.

The Community Services Administration became the publisher of *Federal Outlays* as of the fiscal year 1975 edition. Starting with the fiscal year 1977 edition, the title was changed to the *Geographic Distribution of Federal Funds (GDFF).* Publication of *GDFF* continued through the fiscal year 1980 edition. *GDFF* was discontinued at that time.

## Federal Aid to States

Beginning with fiscal year 1969, *Federal Aid to States (FAS)* was published as a separate document by the Department of the Treasury. Statistics in *FAS* followed the geographic distribution of federal funds to the state level only. *FAS* was primarily concerned with grants-in-aid and did not include federal monies for loan programs, procurement activity, federal salaries and administrative expenses, the Department of State, the Agency for International Development, parts of the Department of Defense, or direct payments to individuals. *FAS* continued as a separate publication through fiscal year 1982. Starting in fiscal year 1983, it was incorporated into *Federal Expenditures by State* as Table 2.

## Annual Report of the Secretary of the Treasury on the State of the Finances

This report did not deal exclusively with the geographic distribution of federal funds. Starting with fiscal year 1929, a separate chart appeared in this document shoeing the distribution of federal funds in broad agency categories to the state level. The chart was published in basically the same format through fiscal year 1968. Its reporting never went beyond the state level.

# Federal Domestic Assistance Programs

## Federal Assistance Awards Data System

The Federal Assistance Awards Data System (FAADS) is an automated system established by the Federal Program Information Act (P.L. 95-220). It contains detailed information on federal monies awarded through the domestic assistance programs listed in the *Catalog of Federal Domestic Assistance*, a comprehensive listing of federal programs which provide financial and non-financial assistance or benefits to the public. The *CFDA* serves as the basic reference source for information on federal domestic assistance programs and contains descriptions of 1,324 programs administered by 53 federal agencies. The *CFDA* is distributed to all federal depository libraries, Members of Congress, and various state offices. Printed copies of the *Catalog* are available for a fee from the Government Printing Office.

Superintendent of Documents
U.S. Government Printing Office
Washington, DC 20402
202/512-1800

It is also available in electronic form on computer disk or CD-ROM. These versions are available from the General Services Administration for a fee.

Federal Domestic Assistance Catalog Staff (MVS)
General Services Administration
Reporters Building, Room 101
300 Seventh Street, SW
Washington, DC 20407
202/708-5126

Access to the *Catalog of Federal Domestic Assistance* is also available on the World Wide Web at http://www.gsa.gov/fdac/.

Searching in the FAADS system can be done by agency name, *CFDA* program number, fiscal year, state, county, city or town, ZIP code, program recipient, and so on. Data are available starting with fiscal year 1981. FAADS computer tapes are distributed by the Department of Commerce, Bureau of the Census. Searching by congressional district is available through the FAADS system.

House offices have access to FAADS data through House Information Resources (HIR) (202/225-6002). HIR offers access through their Post-Award Grants (POST) database. Only the four most recent fiscal quarters available are loaded into the HIR system. House offices should contact HIR for information on access to the POST database and on historical searching.

Senate offices have access to the FAADS data through the Senate Library (202/224-7106), which is connected to the HIR system. The Senate Computer Center also receives copies of the FAADS data tapes. Access to the FAADS data is offered through the Senate Computer Center's Geographic Reporting System (GRS) (202/224-1517). Senate offices can contact the Senate Computer Center for information on historical searching.

Requests for searches of FAADS data through HIR, the Senate Library, the Senate Computer Center, or CRS must be made by Members of Congress or their staff.

Public access to FAADS data is available in different ways. A complete set of FAADS tapes is deposited at the National Archives. Anyone may contact the National Archives to request a copy of magnetic tapes containing the needed data. The National Archives does not actually conduct searches of data. They only supply copies of the magnetic tapes, for a fee.

National Archives
Center for Electronic Records
Reference Service
Room 20E
Washington, DC 20408
202/501-5579

Each state is sent a copy of data tapes shoeing the distribution of monies within its borders. Access to the data in an individual state will vary depending on that state's governmental organization. People wishing to obtain an individual state's data may want to contact the state library to determine the appropriate contact point for their inquiry.

The Bureau of the Census is currently developing a World Wide Web page (http://www.census.gov/pub/govs/www/faads.html) for distribution of FAADS data via the Internet. As of July 1996, the site is under construction.

Members of the public may also contact the office of a Representative or Senator from their state to inquire about FAADS data. Local public libraries with an Internet connection may also be able to provide access to FAADS data once the Census Web site is available.

## FEDERAL PROCUREMENT ACTIVITY

### Federal Procurement Data System

The Federal Procurement Data System (FPDS) was established by the Office of Federal Procurement Policy Act (P.L. 93-400). FPDS is also an automated system and is operated by the General Services Administration (GSA). Collection of data began on October 1, 1978. FPDS contains detailed information on federal procurement activity. Data on individual contracts exceeding $25,000 is required to be included in the system. Contract actions of less than $25,000 are not required to be reported individually in the system. FPDS searching can be done by several different data elements, including agency, date, contractor name and address, city, state, county, kind of contract action, method of solicitation, type of business, and so on. Searches can be tailored to specific fields and are available to the public for a fee.

FPDS is required to collect and compile data only on individual contracts exceeding $25,000. In fiscal year 1995, the federal government entered into approximately 18 million contract actions. Roughly 2.5% (451,000) of these actions exceeded $25,000. However, that small percentage of contract actions accounted for approximately 89% or $181 billion of the $202 billion spent by the federal government on procurement actions during fiscal year 1995. Collecting individual data on the roughly 17.6 million contract actions valued at less than $25,000 each fiscal year is not required at this time. Data is available only in summary form for these contracts.

A statistical overview of federal government procurement activity by state and agency appears in the Bureau of the Census *Federal Expenditures by State* volume. The overview is published as Table 5 and includes all contract actions.

FPDS publishes an annual report titled the *FPDS Federal Procurement Report*. The report presents a summary of federal procurement activity for a given fiscal year. Separate tables providing a list of the top 100 federal contractors, an overview for each federal agency, a federal summary, individual state overviews, an overall state summary, and a summary of contract actions are among items included. The most recent edition of the report is for fiscal year 1995. Copies of the report are available from FPDS. All search requests submitted to FPDS are best done in writing:

U.S. General Services Administration
Federal Procurement Data Center
Seventh and D Streets, SW
ROB Room 5652
Washington, DC 20407

For additional information call 202/401-1529. Congressional offices should identify themselves as such.

A CD-ROM version is available for fiscal year 1994. A fiscal year 1995 edition will be released in August 1996. The CD-ROMs contain data on contracts exceeding $25,000. Searching can be done by agency, Standard Industrial Classification (SIC) codes, state, date, and more. Information on individual contracts valued at less than $25,000 is not available. Contact GSA for information on charges for the CD-ROM versions.

U.S. General Services Administration (MVS)
300 Seventh Street, SW
Reporters Building, Room 101
Washington, DC 20407
202/708-5126

HIR receives copies of the FPDS data and loads them as their Awarded Contracts (AWCO) database. As with FAADS, only data from the four most current fiscal quarters available is loaded into the system. HIR attempts to list the contracts by congressional district where possible and can do searching by congressional district. House offices may contact HIR (225-6002) for further information.

Senate offices may contact the Senate Library (224-7106) for access to the FPDS statistics through the HIR system.

# FEDERAL GRANTS TO STATE AND LOCAL GOVERNMENTS: A BRIEF HISTORY

*Ben Canada*

## EARLY BEGINNINGS AND SLOW DEVELOPMENT

The origins of the grants-in-aid system predate the Constitution. Early grants came in the form of land, as well as funds. The Land Ordinance of 1785, for instance, required every new township incorporated from federal lands to reserve one lot for public schools.[1] The need to help victims of civil disturbance and disasters prompted the federal government to provide assistance to communities. Following the Whiskey Rebellion in late 1794, the federal government compensated individuals who could prove they suffered losses.[2] When the town of Alexandria, Virginia, burned in 1827, Congress quickly appropriated $20,000 in assistance.[3]

In 1790, the federal government set a precedent for federal aid by assuming state Revolutionary War debts. Treasury Secretary Alexander Hamilton proposed the idea, suggesting that it would focus more attention on the national government and establish a sound credit rating for the purposes of future government borrowing. The "anti-federalists," mostly from southern states, hotly contested the idea, arguing that it made the new federal government too centralized, superceded states' rights, and rewarded speculators.[4] Ultimately, the national government assumed the debt, but only after placating the southern states by, among other things, locating the capital city along the Potomac River in the South.[5]

---

1 *Journals of the Continental Congress*, 2nd Continental Congress, p. 378. [http://lcweb2.loc.gov/ammem/amlaw/lwac.html, visited Sept. 18, 2000.]

2 *The Annals of Congress*, 3rd Congress, 2nd Session, pp. 1000-2. [http://lcweb2.loc.gov/ammem/amlaw/lwac.html, visited Sept. 18, 2000.]

3 6 Stat. 356 (1827), Act for The Relief of Indigent Sufferers by The Fire at Alexandria.

4 Many state debt instruments had been purchased at steep discounts by speculators. Hamilton's bill assumed the instruments at full value.

5 Votes on the issue of the permanent seat of government are found in *The Annals of Congress*, First Congress, Second Session, pp. 1039-40, 1735-38. Votes on the issue of assumption of debts are found

While there were occasionally uses of federal grants in the nation's early years, the grants-in-aid system developed very little during the antebellum period. Most efforts to allocate federal funds to state and local governments for internal improvements were either defeated in Congress or vetoed by the President. An exception was the National or Cumberland Road, surveyed and constructed at federal and later, state expense from Cumberland, MD to Vandalia, IL between 1811 and 1850. During this period, states provided virtually all government services, such as education, construction of roads and bridges, and labor regulations. States also had a strong role in policy areas currently viewed as national concerns, such as banks, currency, and business regulation. The national government, conversely, performed few functions. This was largely due to support for states' rights and a strict constructionist approach toward the Constitution – the belief that the national government should only conduct activities expressly granted to it in the Constitution. An example of this philosophy is President Franklin Pierce's veto of an 1854 act, sponsored by reformer Dorothea Dix, to allocate funds to states to help the indigent insane. Pierce contended that if

> Congress is to make provision for [paupers], the fountains of charity will be dried up at home, and the several States, instead of bestowing their own means on the social wants of their people...[will] become humble suppliants for the bounty of the Federal Government, reversing their true relation to this Union.[6]

Early forms of grants-in-aid can be seen in the American migration westward during the 19th century. The movement west greatly depended on aid from federal troops who provided protection from American Indians and constructed a network of over 70 wilderness forts. The forts also provided medical services, blacksmith shops for repairing wagons, and fostered (sometimes created) local economies through supply purchases. Federal assistance also came through its exploration, survey, and road-building efforts. The government also financed postal service, providing communication links to the East.[7]

## THE CIVIL WAR AND THE POST-WAR ERA

The outcome of the Civil War had a significant impact on the future of the grants-in-aid system. The war effectively resolved the long dispute between states' rights advocates, who advocated decentralization, and their opponents, who wanted to make their vision of a unified American nationality a reality. After the War, states' rights advocates lost considerable ground to the view of the Constitution and federal law as

---

at first Congress, Second Session, pp. 1054-55, 1753. [http://lcweb2.loc.gov/ammem/amlaw/lwac.html, visited Sept. 18, 2000.]

6 David B. Walker, *The Rebirth of Federalism: Slouching Toward Washington* (Chatham, NJ: Chatham House Publishers Inc., 1995), pp. 70, 71.

7 John D. Unruh, *The Plains Across: The Overland Emigrants and the Trans-Mississippi West, 1840-60* (Urbana, IL: Univ. of Illinois Press, 1979), pp. 201-243.

supreme law over the states, which set the stage for the development of the grants-in-aid system many years later.[8]

During and immediately following the war, an activist Congress passed several acts that expanded federal involvement in the states. Congress supported westward expansion with the Pacific Railroad Act of 1862, which enabled the government to charter railroad corporations that constructed a transcontinental railroad.[9] The Morril Act of 1862, considered by some observers of federalism as the prototype for future grants-in-aid, provided for the establishment of land-grant universities focusing on agriculture, mechanics, and military science.[10]

Governmental activity at both the state and national level decreased during the years following the Civil War. The 14th Amendment was adopted in 1868 for the purpose of protecting the rights of freed slaves, but the courts interpreted its "due process" clause to be a barrier against state action in social and economic problems. This reduced the states' abilities to respond to new and burgeoning problems generated by the rapid industrialization of the late 19th century. Government inactivity of this period led to the development of philosophies of government intervention and preemption that would later be applied beginning in the 20th century.[11]

President Theodore Roosevelt (1901-1909) used the powers of the Presidency to a greater extent than any of his immediate predecessors. President Roosevelt believed that a strong executive branch was necessary to overcome the "over-division of governmental powers" and address state and local concerns. President Woodrow Wilson (1913-1921) also opposed governmental inactivity by advocating cooperation among federal, state, and local governments. Federal inactivity, however, remained at a relatively low ebb until the 1930s.[12]

## THE NEW DEAL

President Franklin D. Roosevelt's Administration, prompted by the desperate conditions of the Great Depression, accelerated the development of the grants-in-aid system as part of his New Deal program of financial reform, social relief, and economic recovery. It expanded federal involvement in areas where it previously had taken little action, including public housing, health services, and employment security. Soon after taking office, Roosevelt proposed measures that were dependent on a broad constructionist interpretation of the Constitution that would give him flexibility in

---

[8] Alfred H. Kelly, Winfred A. Harbison, and Herman Belz. *The American Constitution: Its Origin and Development*. 6th ed. (New York: W.W. Norton, 1983), pp. 326-7.

[9] Ibid., p. 319.

[10] Ibid., p. 375.

[11] U.S. Advisory Commission on Intergovernmental Relations. *The Condition of Contemporary Federalism: Conflicting Theories and Collapsing Constraints*. (A-78) (Washington: GPO, 1981), p. 60.

[12] Daniel J. Elazar, "The Evolving Federal System," in *The Power to Govern: Assessing Reform in the United States*, Richard Pious ed., *Proceedings of the Academy of Political Science*, vol. 34, 1981. p. 5.

designing economic recovery programs.[13] Examples of New Deal programs still in existence are the Tennessee Valley Authority, which provides electric power and formerly administered infrastructure projects; and Social Security, which provides income security to American workers.[14] The New Deal also extended the use of categorical grant programs, which are currently the most common form of grant. The income tax, authorized by the 16th Amendment in 1913, helped make this expansion of programs possible by providing a continuing and substantial source of income for the federal government.[15] The Supreme Court decisions that upheld New Deal programs also influenced the future of grants by permanently expanding the influence of the federal government into policy areas that had previously been within the states' domain or were not addressed by government at any level.[16]

## GRADUAL EXPANSION OF THE GRANT SYSTEM

The grants-in-aid system expanded gradually during the two decades following the Roosevelt Administration. During the administration of President Harry Truman (1945-1953), the federal government adopted grant programs in several areas, including agricultural research, health initiatives, and urban improvements.[17] In 1949, the Hoover Commission[18] made the first recommendation for block grants, stating that "a system of grants be established based upon broad categories – such as highways, education, public assistance, and public health – as contrasted with the present system of extensive fragmentation." Despite this recommendation, Congress did not create a block grant until 1966 - the Partnership for Public Health. The number of grant programs further expanded during the administration of President Dwight Eisenhower (1953-1961).[19] By the time Eisenhower left office, total grant outlays had nearly tripled, from $2.4 billion to $6.8 billion. The interstate highway system is one of the programs begun under this administration.[20]

Use of the grants mechanism vastly increased during the administration of President Lyndon Johnson (1963-1969). Relying implicitly on the Fourteenth Amendment and the commerce clause in the Constitution, Congress and the President enacted legislation that established new approaches to achieving national goals. Johnson's "Great Society" programs extended federal involvement in state and local government, as these sub-national governments began implementing federal programs. These programs focused on

---

[13] Kelly, *The American Constitution*, p. 482.

[14] Walker, *The Rebirth of Federalism*, pp. 94-95.

[15] Ibid., p. 33.

[16] Ibid., pp. 94-95.

[17] Ibid., p. 103.

[18] One of two presidentially appointed study commissions chaired by former President Herbert Hoover. The commissions proposed executive branch procedural and administrative reforms.

[19] Carl W. Stenberg and David B. Walker. Advisory Commission on Intergovernmental Relations. *The Block Grant: Lessons from Two Early Experiments*. Publius v. 7, Spring 1977. p. 31.

[20] David B. Walker, *The Rebirth of Federalism*, p. 103.

urban and metropolitan areas, as well as the needs of minority and disadvantaged populations. More grant programs were enacted during Johnson's five years than in all preceding year in U.S. history. All of the new programs were categorical grants, with the exception of two block grants in the fields of health and law enforcement.[21] Total grant outlays nearly doubled between 1964 and 1968, from $10.1 billion to $18.6 billion.[22]

## CHANGES IN THE SYSTEM: NIXON AND REAGAN

The expansion of grants-in-aid under Johnson led to a call for reform under President Richard Nixon (1969-1974). Nixon characterized the system as a "terrible tangle" of categorical grants plagued by overlapping programs, inefficiency, excessive administrative requirements, and imposition of federal priorities on state and local governments.[23] His primary goals were to improve program efficiency, decentralize decision-making to states and localities, and restrain program growth.

Nixon advocated the use of general revenue sharing and special revenue sharing to achieve these goals.[24] General revenue sharing sent funds to states and local governments with virtually no programmatic requirements. The goal of general revenue sharing was to combine the advantages of national revenue collection with the advantages of local discretion over spending.[25] Representative Melvin Laird (R-WI), was a pioneer in the field, introduced a revenue sharing bill as early as 1958. Walter Heller, Chairman of the council of Economic Advisers in the Kennedy and Johnson administrations, proposed general revenue sharing in 1960 as a potential use of federal surpluses, but his plan received little attention until the Nixon Administration.[26] The program distributed funds to states from 1972-81 and to local governments from 1972-86, but was not re-authorized in 1986 as part of efforts to control mounting deficits.[27] Nixon also proposed special revenue sharing, which merged the funding of functionally related categorical programs into large allocations distributed to states. He intended to give the states broad discretion in addressing the functional area.[28] Special revenue sharing functioned similarly to block grants, but required no application and had fewer programmatic strings. Congress, however, favored block grants over special revenue sharing and modified most of

---

[21] Ibid., pp. 132-133.

[22] Advisory Commission on Intergovernmental Relations, *Significant Features of Fiscal Federalism, 1985-1986* (Washington: GPO, 1986), p. 19.

[23] William Lilley III, Timothy B. Clark, and John K. Iglehart. New Federalism Report/Nixon attack on grant programs aims to simplify structure, give greater local control. National Journal. vol. 5, Jan. 20, 1973. p. 76.

[24] Timothy Conlan, *From New Federalism to Devolution: Twenty-five Years of Intergovernmental Reform* (Washington: Brookings Institution Press, 1998), p. 19-21.

[25] Ibid., p. 65.

[26] Michael Reagan, *The New Federalism* (New York: Oxford Univ. Press, 1972), pp. 89-90.

[27] Advisory Commission on Intergovernmental Relations, *Characteristics of Federal Grant-in-aid Programs (Washington: GPO, 1994), p. iii.*

[28] Reagan, *The New Federalism*, p. 60.

Nixon's special revenue sharing proposals to block grant programs. One such Nixon proposal was adopted as the Community Development Block Grant program (CDBG).[29]

Although Nixon intended to devolve a greater degree of decision-making to states and localities, the changes that occurred during his administration ultimately expanded federal intervention into state and local governments. The new block grants and revenue sharing gave the federal government more influence over state and local policy-making because the federal government placed conditions on the use of funds. Funds could be reduced or withheld if the recipient government failed to meet these conditions. Since block grants and general revenue sharing brought federal aid into many communities for the first time, "New Federalism" enabled the federal government to have more influence over American society than ever before.[30]

The administration of President Ronald Reagan (1981-1989) also pushed for grant reform. Reagan's efforts differed from those of Nixon in that Reagan not only wanted to decentralize grant administration to state and local governments, but also reduce funding and alter priorities in the grants-in-aid system. Reagan wanted to reduce federal government regulatory power that had developed through expansion of the grant system. He supported the block grant as a means of both disengaging the national government from policy areas he viewed as state and local concerns and of reducing spending.[31] Reagan was initially successful in his efforts. The Omnibus Budget Reconciliation Act (OBRA) of 1981 consolidated 77 categorical programs into nine block grants. OBRA reduced total grant outlays to state and local governments by $6 billion below the previous fiscal year. Most of the budget cuts came in the areas of education, job training, and welfare. There was, however, little change after the first two years of his administration. The growth rate of the grants-in-aid system slowed during the Reagan years, but did not halt.[32]

## RECENT DEVELOPMENTS

The Supreme Court upheld the practice of conditioning grants in its 1987 ruling on *South Dakota v. Dole*. South Dakota challenged the ability of the federal government to withhold federal highway funds from states with drinking ages below 21 years of age. The court ruled that Congress could use its spending power to encourage uniformity in the states' drinking ages. Further, it ruled that "Congress may attach conditions on the receipt of federal funds. However, exercise of the power is subject to certain restrictions, including that it must be in pursuit of 'the general welfare.'"[33]

---

[29] *Congressional Record,* vol. 119. 93rd Congress, 1st Session. p. 39377-81.

[30] Conlan, *From New Federalism to Devolution*, 85-87.

[31] Ibid., pp. 142-144.

[32] Ibid., p. 114.

[33] U.S. Supreme Court. *South Dakota v. Dole*, 483 U.S. 203 (1987). [http://caselaw.findlaw.com/scripts/getcase.pl?court=us&vol=483&invol=203, Visited Aug. 14, 2000.]

Not all Supreme Court decisions have upheld federal grant practices. In fact, during the 1990s, many court rulings have limited federal power over the states. An example is the 1995 ruling in *United States v. Lopez*. Here, the court ruled unconstitutional the Gun-Free School Zones Act, which made it a federal offense to possess a firearm within 1000 feet of a school. The court deemed the Act exceeded Congress' commerce clause authority, since possession of a gun in a school zone is not an activity that substantially affects interstate commerce.[34]

The grants-in-aid system has seen little change under the Bush and Clinton administrations. President George Bush attempted to consolidate several categorical programs into larger, lower-funded block programs; but Congress failed to act on his proposals.[35] President Bill Clinton's National Performance Review (NPR) focused on improving governmental management and performance. The NPR implied greater state and local flexibility over grant programs, but with the understanding that the federal government would closely monitor the performance of the programs. Some observers have rated the NPR as having a minor impact on the grants-in-aid system.[36]

The 104th Congress (1995-1997) proposed many reforms that would have consolidated categorical programs into block grant programs, but most of these reforms were never passed. Seventy-three small grant programs were eliminated, but these comprised only $2.3 billion in funding cuts. Arguable among the most significant reform passed by the 104th Congress was the conversion of the open-ended entitlement grant, Aid to Families with Dependent Children (AFDC), to a capped block grant called Temporary Assistance to Needy Families (TANF). While the accomplishments of TANF continue to be debated, the program represents the most recent major reform of the grants-in-aid system.[37]

While there have been few major reform attempts since the early 1980s, future Congresses and Presidents may modify the grants-in-aid system to respond to the ever-changing needs of society generally, and state and local governments in particular.

---

[34] U.S. Supreme Court, *United States v. Lopez*, No. 93-1260.
[35] Walker, *The Rebirth of Federalism*. pp. 162-165.
[36] Conlan, *From New Federalism to Devolution*. pp. 221-224.
[37] Ibid., pp. 243-251.

# COMMUNITY DEVELOPMENT BLOCK GRANTS: FUNDING AND OTHER ISSUES IN THE 106$^{TH}$ CONGRESS

*Eugene Boyd*

## BACKGROUND AND ANALYSIS

The CDBG program is the largest source of federal financial assistance in support of housing, neighborhood revitalization, and community and economic development efforts of state and local governments. The Administration's CDBG budget request of $4.9 billion for FY2001 would provide $250 million more to entitlement communities and states under the formula component of the program than the $4.236 allocated to entitlement communities and states for FY2000. This proposed increase would be achieved by increasing overall CDBG spending by $119 million and reducing total CDBG set-asides by $131 million.

### Community Development Block Grant Appropriations for FY2001

The Clinton Administration's FY2001 budget proposal for the Community Development Block Grants (CDBG) totaled $4.9 billion, including $414 million for program set-asides. This was $100 million more than originally appropriated for FY2000, and $119 million more after subtracting the mandatory 0.38% cut in discretionary spending as required by the Consolidated Appropriations Act of 2000, P.L. 106-113. The conference version of H.R. 4635, appropriates $5.058 billion for CDBG activities, including $649 million for program set-asides.

The Administration proposed several new initiatives under the CDBG program, the two most notable being $22 million for a community and economic development initiative in the Mississippi Delta, and $20 million for a technical assistance and capacity building program for faith-based organizations involved in community and economic development efforts. The final version of H.R. 4635 did not include funding for the Youthbuild program ($75 million) and for capacity building grants to community development corporations and nonprofit housing organizations ($24 million). The final version of H.R. 4635 appropriates $60 million for Youthbuild, less than requested by the Administration, but $17 million more than appropriated in FY2000. The Youthbuild program, which funds training and apprenticeship programs in construction trades for young adults involved in low income housing construction and rehabilitation projects, is the second largest set-aside under the CDBG program. The conference version of the act also increased funding for capacity building grants to community development corporations and nonprofit housing organizations to $28 million, $8 million more than appropriated in FY2000.

These and other CDBG-based initiatives would have been offset by eliminating or reducing funding for a number of other CDBG set-asides, including:

- Supportive Services Grants ($55 million in FY2000);
- Neighborhood Initiative Grants ($30 million for FY2000); and
- Economic Development Initiative (EDI) Grants ($256 million in FY2000 earmarks).

Instead Congress approved $649 million in set-asides, including $55 million for Supportive Services Grants; $44 million for Neighborhood Initiative Grants; and $292 million for EDI grants.

The largest CDBG set-aside is the Economic Development Initiative (EDI) program. These funds are used in conjunction with Section 108 loan guarantees to fund economic development projects. EDI (Sec. 108(q)) grants have been used in the past by Members of Congress to fund specific projects. In FY2000, Members of Congress earmarked 87% of these grants for specific projects. For FY1999, Congress earmarked 82% ($185 million) of the $225 million in EDI appropriations for specific projects identified in the conference report accompanying the FY1999 VA, HUD, and Independent Agencies Appropriations Act.

The Administration and entitlement communities and states have objected to EDI earmarks on the grounds that they are noncompetitive. They have argued that large EDI earmarks reduce the amount of funds available under the core CDBG program for distribution to entitlement communities and states. For FY2000, approximately $232 million of the $256 million in EDI assistance was earmarked for specific projects identified in the conference report accompanying the VA-HUD-Independent Agencies Appropriations Act.

## Table 1. CDBG Funding: FY2000 Actual and FY2001 Proposed

| Program | FY2000 Actual | FY2001 Appropriations Request | | | |
|---|---|---|---|---|---|
| | | Admin. | House | Senate | Confer. |
| **CDBG Total** | **$4,800.0** | **$4,900.0** | **$4,505.0** | **$4,800.0** | **$5,058.0** |
| Entitlement | 2,965.2 | 3,140.2 | 2,949.8 | 3,087.9 | 3,086.3 |
| States | 1,270.8 | 1,345.8 | 1,264.2 | 1,323.4 | 1,322.7 |
| **Total Set-Asides** | **545.0** | **414.0** | **291.0** | **388.7** | **649.0** |
| Indian Tribes | 67.0 | 69.0 | 67.0 | 67.0 | 71.0 |
| Native Amer. Econ. Dev. Access Center | -- | [2.0] | 0.0 | 0.0 | 0.0 |
| Tribal Colleges and Universities | -- | [5.0] | 0.0 | 3.0 | -[b] |
| National Amer. Indian Housing Council | 2.2 | 2.2 | 3.0 | 2.2 | 2.6 |
| Housing Assistance Counsel | 3.0 | 3.0 | 3.0 | 3.0 | 3.0 |
| Sec. 107 | 41.5 | 68.5 | 39.5 | 41.5 | 45.5 |
| New Market University Partnership | -- | [5.0] | 0.0 | 0.0 | 0.0 |
| Institutions serving Native Alaskans and Hawaiians | [2.0] | [2.0] | 0.0 | [3.0] | [3.0] |
| National Housing Development Corp. | -- | -- | -- | -- | 10.0 |
| Self-help Housing Opportunity Program | 24.0 | 17.5 | 20.0 | 0.0 | 20.0 |
| Mississippi Delta Region Initiative | -- | 22.0 | 0.0 | 0.0 | 0.0 |
| Capacity Building for Com. Dev. And Affordable Housing | 23.75 | 31.5[a] | 23.75 | 25.0[a] | 28.45[a] |
| National Comm. Dev. Initiative | [20] | [24.0] | [20.0] | [20.0] | [20.0] |
| Rural and tribal areas | [4.0] | [4.0] | [4.0] | [5.0] | [5.0] |
| Habitat for Humanities Cap. Building | [3.75] | [7.5] | [3.75] | -- | [3.45] |
| Supportive Services | 55.0 | -- | 55.0 | 55.0 | 55.0 |
| Neighborhood Initiative | 30.0 | -- | 10.0 | 0.0 | 44.0 |
| Earmarked projects | [23.0] | -- | 0.0 | 0.0 | [44.0] |
| Youthbuild | 42.5 | 75.0 | 45.0 | 60.0 | 60.0 |
| Youthbuild USA for capacity-building | [2.5] | [3.75] | [3.75] | [4.0] | [4.0] |
| Youthbuild for underserved and rural areas | -- | -- | -- | [10.0] | [10.0] |
| Econ. Dev. Initiative (EDI) Sec. 108(q) | 275.0 | 100.0 | 10.0 | 130.0 | 292.0 |
| EDI earmarks | [240.0] | -- | 0.0 | [123.0] | [292.0] |
| Faith and community-based non-profits capacity-building and technical assistance | -- | 20.0 | 0.0 | 0.0 | 0.0 |
| Working Cap. Fund for Info. Tech. Systems | -- | -- | -- | -- | 15.0 |
| Salt Lake City Olympic Games Temporary Housing | -- | -- | -- | -- | 2.0 |
| Other | 9.75 | 9.5 | 15.0 | 2.0 | 0.0 |
| Total | $4,871.0 | $4,900.0 | $4,505.0 | $4,800.0 | $5,058.0 |
| Sec. 108 Loan Guarantee Subsidy | 29.0 | 28.0 | 28.0 | 29.0 | 29.0 |

[a] Includes funding for LISC and Enterprise Foundation for activities that supports capacity-building and technical assistance to community development corporations and community housing development organizations.
[b] $3 million in funding for this activity is included under Section 107 grants.
Note: Totals may not add up due to rounding. Brackets indicate amount subsumed under line immediately above.

*Funding for Capacity Building Initiatives*

For FY2000, Congress set aside $25 million in CDBG funds for capacity building activities intended to help nonprofit organizations obtain the training necessary to effectively:

- compete for grants;
- administer federal assistance programs; and
- implement neighborhood improvement programs.

Capacity building and technical assistance increasingly have become a focus of the Department of Housing and Urban Development in its efforts to develop partnerships with, and provide nonprofit entities including community development corporations, housing developers, and faith-based institutions with greater access to HUD programs. For FY2001, the Administration is requesting a 120% increase in funding for capacity building under the CDBG program. This includes $20 million to finance a new program in support of faith-based institutions and $7.75 million increase in funding for capacity building assistance targeted to community development corporations and nonprofit housing entities. Three national intermediaries – Local Initiative Support Corporation (LISC) at [www.liscnet.org], the Enterprise Foundation at [www.enterprisefoundation.org], and Habitat for Humanity International at [www.habitat.org] – have annual set asides to carry out capacity building activities.

The House-passed version of H.R. 4635, the VA, HUD, Independent Agencies Appropriations Act for FY2001, included $27.5 million in direct CDBG assistance for capacity building and technical assistance activities (See Table 2). This is $2.25 million more than appropriated in FY2000. The Senate recommended slightly higher funding of $29 million. The final conference version of H.R. 4635, which was forwarded to the President on October 19, 2000, includes $32 million in direct CDBG assistance for capacity building and technical assistance activities. This is less than the $55 million the Administration was seeking for these activities.

**Table 2. CDBG Set-asides and Earmarked Funding for Capacity Building Activities (in millions of dollars)**

| Program | FY2000 Actual | FY2001 Appropriations Request | | | |
|---|---|---|---|---|---|
| | | Admin. | House | Senate | Confer. |
| Capacity Building for Com. Dev. And Affordable Housing | 23.75 | 31.5 | 23.75 | 25.0 | 28.0 |
| National Comm. Dev. Initiative | [20.0] | [24.0] | [20.0] | [20.0] | [20.0] |
| Rural and tribal areas | [4.0] | [4.0] | [4.0] | [4.0] | [5.0] |
| Habitat for Humanities Cap. Building | [3.75] | [7.5] | [3.75] | -- | [3.45] |
| Youthbuild USA Capacity Building | 2.5 | 3.75 | 3.75 | 4.0 | 4.0 |
| Cap. Building and Tech. Assist. For Faith-based Nonprofits | -- | 20.0 | 0.0 | 0.0 | 0.0 |
| Total | $25.25 | $55.25 | $27.5 | $29.0 | $32.0 |

Note: Total may not add due to rounding. Brackets indicate amount subsumed under line immediately above.

## Related Programs and Proposals

*Regional Connections*

The Administration's FY2001 budget includes $25 million in support of smart growth initiatives intended to mitigate the impacts of suburban sprawl and promote regional strategies for land use development. The grant program, which is a part of the Administration's "livability agenda," would be administered by states or regional organizations such as Councils of Government (COGs) or Metropolitan Planning Organizations (MPOs). According to the Administration, the program's core purpose would be to promote and coordinate regional solutions to infrastructure development, transportation planning, and workforce development. The Administration's FY2000 budget proposal included $50 million for a Regional Connections Program, which failed to win congressional support. Neither the conference, House or Senate versions of H.R. 4635, the VA, HUD, Independent Agencies Act for FY2001, including funding for the Regional Connections Program.

*America's Private Investment Companies (APICs)*

The program would be administered by the HUD and Small Business Administration (SBA). Modeled after SBA's Small Business Investment Companies (SMIC) program, the APIC program is intended to encourage equity investment in large-scale development projects in economically distressed urban and rural communities. The program is expected to leverage $278 million in private equity investments. The Administration's FY2001 budget request includes $37 million in tax credits, which are expected to leverage $1 billion in private investment. For FY2000 the Congress appropriated $20 million in credit subsidies to support $556 million in loan guarantees.

The VA-HUD-Independent Agencies Appropriations Act for FY2000, P.L. 106-74, includes $20 million for APICs, pending enactment of authorizing legislation by June 30, 2000. If legislation is not enacted, funds would be transferred to the Community Development Financial Institutions program at the Department of Treasury.

Legislators made some progress in meeting the June 30, 2000 deadline for enactment of APIC authorizing legislation. On April 13, 2000, the House Banking and Financial Services Committee reported H.R.2764, America's Private Investment Companies Act. The bill, which was introduced on September 9, 1999, was discharged from the House Subcommittee on Housing and Community Opportunity on April 12, 2000. It was considered, marked up, and reported out of full committee the next day. During the committee's consideration of the bill, an amendment was added that would limit program authorization to 5 years. During this 5-year period, HUD would license 15 new for-profit APICs annually. After several weeks of negotiations between the Administration and the Speaker of the House, the House considered and passed H.R.4923, the Community Renewal and New Markets Act of 2000. A similar measure, S.2779, was introduced in the Senate on June 22, 2000. Both bills would authorize the creation of APICs.

The report (H.Rept. 106-1005) accompanying the conference version of H.R. 4635- the VA, HUD, Independent Agencies Appropriations bill for FY2001 – pledges $37 million in tax credits for APICs upon Congress passing the President's New Market Initiative legislation. The House version of H.R. 4635 does not include funding for the APIC program. H.Rept. 106-674 accompanying H.R.4635 noted the absence of legislation authorizing the creation of APICs as the reason for not funding the APIC program. The Senate Appropriations Committee version of H.R. 4635 does not include funding for APICs.

*Brownfield Redevelopment*

Brownfields are contaminated industrial and commercial facilities. Developers of designated brownfield sites may receive federal funds, including Environmental Protection Agency funds, to remove or mitigate the effects of the environmental contaminants. Other funds, including brownfield funds administered by HUD, may be used to assist in redeveloping the site or facility for new commercial or industrial uses.

HUD is requesting $50 million in funding for brownfield redevelopment projects. This is $25 million more than appropriated in FY2000. HUD funds would be used to finance job creation activities that benefit low and moderate-income persons. Administration estimates place the number of eligible brownfield sites at 450,000 nationwide. HUD funds are used in conjunction with Section 108 loan guarantees, and are expected to leverage $200 million in Section108 commitments, which could support the creation of 20,000 to 25,000 jobs, according to administration estimates.

The House-passed version of H.R. 4635, the VA, HUD, Independent Agencies Appropriations Act for FY2001, includes $20 million in funding for brownfield redevelopment projects. Such projects would fund EDI grants and could leverage additional funds through the use of Sec. 108 loan guarantees. The conference version of H.R. 4635 includes $25 million for brownfield redevelopment. The same amount recommended by the Senate.

*Empowerment Zones and Enterprise Communities (EZs/ECs)*

The EZ/EC program provides targeted tax incentives and grants to selected urban and rural cities and counties. Federal assistance is used to encourage private sector economic activity in economically distressed urban neighborhoods and rural areas leading to job opportunities for residents of the area, particularly low- and moderate-income residents. In 1994, HUD and U.S. Department of Agriculture (USDA) created 104 EZs/ECs in urban and rural areas. In 1999, a second group (Round (II) of communities (15 urban/5 rural) received the EZ designation. For FY2000, Congress appropriated $55 million for the 20 EZs designated in 1999. The Administration requested an additional $55 million for FY2001 for these Round II EZs. Neither the House nor Senate version of H.R. 4635, the VA, HUD, Independent Agencies Act for FY2001, includes funding for EZ/ECs. However, the conference version of the act includes $90 million for Round II empowerment zones, including $75 million for urban zones and $15 million on rural zones. The conference report pledges an additional $110 million for EZs should Congress pass New Market legislation.

**Table 3. CDBG-Related Programs (in millions of dollars)**

| Program | FY2000 Approp. | Proposed Appropriations | | | Conf. |
|---|---|---|---|---|---|
| | | Adm. | House | Senate | |
| Regional Connections | -- | 25.0 | 0.0 | 0.0 | 0.0 |
| Empowerment Zones | 55.0 | 55.0 | 0.0 | 0.0 | 90.0 |
| Brownfield Redevelopment | 25.0 | 50.0 | 20.0 | 25.0 | 25.0 |
| America's Private Investment Companies | 20.0 | 37.0 | 0.0 | 0.0 | 0.0 |
| Total | $100.0 | $167.0 | 20.0 | 25.0 | $115.0 |

## H.R. 1776: Reauthorizing and Amending the CDBG Program

On April 12, 2000, the House passed H.R. 1776, the American Homeownership and Economic Opportunity Act of 2000. The bill includes CDBG-related provisions that would:

- authorize the program for 5 years, from FY2001 through FY2005;
- modify the income targeting requirements of the program; and
- limit the number of the CDBG-linked set-asides.

*Proposed Revision in the Income Targeting of CDBG Funds*

The CDBG program requires that 70% of the allocation awarded to each entitlement community or state be used to fund activities that benefit low-and moderate-income persons.[12] The bill includes a provision intended to encourage home ownership among municipal workers. For the purpose of promoting home ownership among teachers and uniformed municipal employees (including policemen, firemen, and sanitation and other maintenance workers), the bill would allow local governments to increase to 115% (150% in high housing costs areas) the income ceiling governing the definition of low- and moderate-income families and persons. The bill would amend the list of eligible activities to include:

- mortgage down payments;
- reasonable closing costs normally associated with the purchase of a residence;
- pre- or post-purchase counseling on the financial and other obligations of home ownership; or mortgage interest rates subsidy.

Supporters of the amendment argue that a home ownership program for first time homebuyers, would encourage eligible municipal employees to consider residing within the jurisdiction where they are employed. This incentive is a means of combating the flight of civic leadership and middle-class tax dollars to adjacent jurisdictions. Opponents of the provision argue that it reduces the funds available for the truly needy. In addition, the program, which would be limited to uniformed municipal employees and teachers, would result in unequal treatment of other non-uniformed municipal employees.

---

[1] Low-and moderate-income families and individuals are those whose income does not exceed 80% of the median income of the area involved. 42 U.S.C. 5302(a)(20)(A).

[2] Low-and moderate-income families and individuals are those whose income does not exceed 80% of the median income for the area involved. 42 U.S.C. 5302(a)(20)(A).

*Limiting the Use of Set-asides under the CDBG Program*

The bill, H.R. 1776, would prohibit the use of set-asides, except for Indian tribes, and special purpose grants authorized under 42 U.S.C. 5307. These include grants:

- to Guam, Virgin Islands, American Samoa, and the Commonwealth of the Northern Mariana Islands; to historically black colleges and universities;
- to community development work study program;
- to colleges and universities in partnership with states and local governments;
- for community adjustment and economic diversification activities stemming from military base closures; and for technical assistance to state and local governments.

The bill would allocate the remaining funds by formula to states and entitlement communities. It would also require that any amendment or appropriation language that would violate the provision limiting the use of set-asides must specifically refer to subsection 408(b) of the Housing and Economic Opportunity Act of 2000, H.R. 1776, currently under consideration in the House; and state that the amendment or appropriation provision modifies or supersedes subsection 408(b).

The bill would exclude Sec. 108 financed projects from the requirements of Sec. 4078(b). (See Table 4)

Subsection 408(b) would not cover CDBG set-asides under Section 108, the provision governing loan guarantees and Economic Development Initiative grants. As presently structured, the provision would allow Members to request earmarks under subsection 108(q) of Title I of the Housing and Community Development Act of 1974, 42 U.S.C. 5308(q). In FY2000, EDIs comprised 50.4% of total CDBG set-asides, specific EDI earmarks actually accounted for 44% of total CDBG set-asides. The remaining 6.4% of funds were allocated for competitively awarded EDI funds (See Chart 1). Proponents of set-asides content that such projects serve as demonstration and models that test the applicability of certain activities and approaches. Critics of set-asides argue that:

- they siphon funds form the core program – CDBG's formula-based block grants;
- they are narrowly focused categorical programs hidden within a block grant; and they are awarded non-competitively to specific projects.

## Table 4. CDBG Set-Asides (in millions of dollars)

| | FY2000 Actual | FY2001 Proposed | | | |
|---|---|---|---|---|---|
| | | Admin. | House | Sen. | Confer. |
| **Total Set-asides** | **545.0** | **414.0** | **291.0** | **387.9** | **649.0** |
| Indian Tribes | 67.0 | 69.0 | 67.0 | 67.0 | 71.0 |
| Sec. 107 | 41.5 | 68.5 | 39.5 | 41.5 | 45.5 |
| Subtotal | 108.5 | 137.5 | 106.5 | 108.5 | 116.5 |
| **Set-asides that would be in noncompliance with Subsection 408(b) of H.R. 1776** | | | | | |
| Self-Help Housing Opportunity Program | 20.0 | 17.5 | 20.0 | 0.0 | 20.0 |
| Mississippi Delta Region Initiative | -- | 22.0 | 0.0 | 0.0 | 0.0 |
| Capacity Building for Com. Dev. And Affordable Housing | 23.7 | 31.5[a] | 23.4 | 25.0 | 28.0 |
| Supportive Services | 55.0 | -- | 55.0 | 55.0 | 55.0 |
| Neighborhood Initiative | 30.0 | -- | 10.0 | 0.0 | 44.0 |
| Youthbuild | 42.5 | 75.0 | 45.0 | 60.0 | 60.0 |
| Faith-based non-profits capacity-building and technical assistance[1] | -- | 20.0 | 0.0 | 0.0 | 0.0 |
| Other | 9.7 | 9.5 | 21.0 | 9.4 | 33.5 |
| Subtotal | 161.5 | 176.5 | 174.4 | 149.4 | 236.6 |
| **Set-asides not subject to subsection 408(b) prohibition** | | | | | |
| Econ. Dev. Initiative (EDI) Sec. 108(q) | 35.0 | 100.0 | 10.0 | 7.0 | 0.0 |
| EDI earmarks (sec 108q)[a] | 240.0 | -- | 0.0 | 123.0 | 292.0 |

[a] Does not include $20 million for brownfield redevelopment activities.

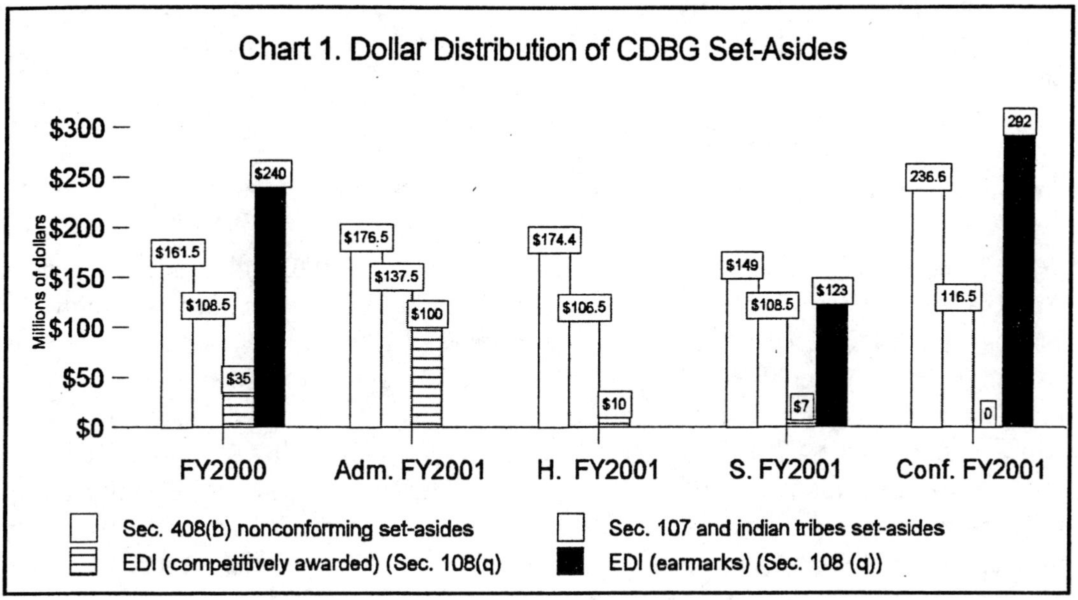


## Optional Entitlement Communities (OECs)

Late in the first session of the 106th Congress, HUD unveiled a proposal that would create a new category of entitlement community eligible for a direct formula-based allocation of funds. The new category, called optional entitlement communities (OECs), would include:

- cities with population of 25,000 to 49,999; and
- counties with populations between 100,000 and 200,000.

Communities meeting these thresholds – 263 cities and 159 counties according 1998 Census estimates – would receive formula-based allocations directly from HUD. Funding for an OEC that have no OECs would experience no change in their formula allocation. OECs in each state would receive a formula allocation equal to the OEC's share of the state's formula allocation. For example, if an OEC's formula factors account for 5% of a state's formula allocation, the OEC would receive a direct allocation of 5% of the state's non-entitlement allocation. The state's non-entitlement allocation would be reduced by a corresponding amount.

Supporters content that the proposal would provide a predictable stream of funds, increase local control over the distribution of funds, and improve the long-range community planning function. Detractors counter that the proposal would reduce the amount of funds available to smaller and poorer communities whose populations do not meet the OEC thresholds, reduce the role of the state in community planning, and further fragment HUD's delivery of services. In addition, critics content that the OECs would further strain HUD's ability to manage and oversee the entitlement communities program.

### Community Development Appropriations for FY2000

On October 20, 1999, the President signed the VA-HUD-Independent Agencies Appropriations Act for FY2000 into law as P.L. 106-74. The act included $4.8 million in funding for CDBG activities. On December 23, 1999, the President signed the Consolidated Appropriations Act for FY2000, P.L. 106-113. This act included a mandatory 0.38% across-the-board cut in discretionary spending; as a result the CDBG appropriation was $4.781 billion. Approximately 11.4% of total CDBG funds are allocated to set-asides. Of the $545 million allocated for set-asides in FY2000, nearly 45% ($240 million) is allocated to Section 108(q) EDI earmarks. These are for specific projects identified in the conference report (H.Rept. 106-379), which must be funded under the Section 108(q) provision.

## LEGISLATION

**H.R. 1776 (Lazio)**

American Homeownership and Economic Opportunity Act of 2000. A bill to expand home ownership in the United States and for other purposes. Passed House April 6, 2000 (Roll Call Vote 110: Yea and Nays: 417-8).

**H.R. 2764 (LaFalce)**

A bill to license America's Private Investment Companies and provide enhanced credit to stimulate private investment in low-income communities, and for other purposes. House Committee on Banking and Financial Services ordered the bill to be reported (amended) April 13, 2000.

**H.R. 4635 (Walsh)**

A bill to provide appropriations for activities of the Departments of Veteran Affairs, Housing and Urban Development, and Independent Agencies for FY2001. House Committee on Appropriations reported on original measure, H.R. 4635 (H.Rept. 106-67) June 12. 2000.

## CONGRESSIONAL HEARINGS, REPORTS, AND DOCUMENTS

U.S. Congress. House. Committee on Appropriations. H.Rept. 106-674 to accompany H.R. 4635, Departments of Veteran Affairs, Housing and Urban Development Appropriations Act for FY2001. June 12, 2000.

---H.Rept. 106-1005 to accompany H.R. 4635, Department of Veteran Affairs, Housing and Urban Development Appropriations Act for FY2001, October 18, 2000.

U.S. Congress. House. Committee on Banking and Financial Services, H.Rept. 106-553 to accompany H.R. 1776, American Homeownership and Economic Opportunity Act of 2000. April 5, 2000.

---H.Rept. 106-638 to accompany H.R. 2764, America's Private Investment Companies Act of 2000. May 23, 2000.

U.S. Congress. Senate. Committee on Appropriations. S.Rept. 106-410 to accompany H.R. 4635, Departments of Veteran Affairs, Housing and Urban Development Appropriations Act for FY2001. Sept. 13, 2000.

## CHRONOLOGY

**10/19/2000** House agrees to the conference report by the Yeas and Nays: 386-24 (Roll no. 536).

Senate agreed to conference report by Yea-Nay Vote. 85-8. Record Vote Number: 278.

**10/18/2000** Conference report H.Rept. 106-988 filed.

**10/12/2000** Passed Senate with an amendment by Yea-Nay Vote. 87-8. Record Vote Number: 272

**09/13/2000** H.R. 4635 reported by the Senate Appropriations Committee (S.Rept. 106-410).

**06/21/2000** H.R. 4635 passed by the House. Measure agreed to by recorded vote: 256-169 (Roll Call Vote 309).

**06/12/2000** House Committee on Appropriations reported an original measure, H.R. 4635 (H.Rept. 106-674).

**05/23/2000** H.R. 2764 reported (amended) by Committee on Banking and Financial Services (H.Rept. 106-638).

**04/13/2000** H.R. 2764 ordered reported (amended) by the Yeas and Nays: 33-14.

**04/06/2000** H.R. 1776 passed by House. House agreed to by recorded vote: 417-8 (Roll Call Vote 110).

**03/29/2000** H.R. 1776 reported (amended) by Committee on Banking and Financial Services (H.Rept. 106-553). Ordered reported by voice vote.

**08/05/1999** H.R. 2764 introduced and referred to House Committee on Banking and Financial Services.

**05/12/1999** H.R. 1776 introduced and referred to House Committee on Banking and Financial Services.

# STATE AND LOCAL ECONOMIC SANCTIONS: SOME CONSTITUTIONAL ISSUES

*Jeanne J. Grimmett*

Increasingly, states and localities have proposed or enacted measures restricting governmental transactions with firms doing business or having financial ties with foreign countries whose conduct the state or locality has found objectionable, particularly in the human rights area. This report summarizes some constitutional arguments made for and against these laws and discusses *Crosby v. National Foreign Trade Council*, the June 19, 2000, U.S. Supreme Court decision holding that the Massachusetts law restricting state transactions with firms doing business with Burma was preempted by federal Burma sanctions and that is application was unconstitutional under the Supremacy Clause.[1]

## DESCRIPTIONS OF STATE AND LOCAL SANCTIONS LAWS

State and local sanctions measures have generally taken the form of: (1) selective purchasing or contracting laws, which generally prohibit state or local agencies from contracting with or procuring goods and services from companies that do business in a named country, or (2) selective investment laws, which prohibit states or local agencies from investing public funds in such companies. A variation of the latter is the state or local divestment law, which may require the divestment of, *e.g.*, state and employee pension funds from companies that do business with or in a named country. State and

---

[1] Opinion available at [http://www.supremecourtus.gov/opinions/99oplist.html]. Selective procurement laws have also raised questions as to their consistency with U.S. obligations under the World Trade Organization (WTO) Agreement on Government Procurement (AGP), which covers purchases by certain state agencies, including those in Massachusetts. On October 21, 1998, the WTO Dispute Settlement Body established a panel to examine complaints by the European Union and Japan that the Massachusetts law violates various AGP provisions. Panel proceedings were suspended at complainants' request in February 1999 following the district court decision in the *Crosby* case; the panel's authority lapsed as of February 11, 2000, pursuant to WTO rules.

local sanctions laws vary as to their scope and countries targeted by the measures. According to one source, as of January 2000, two states and 26 localities had enacted either selected purchasing or investment laws (or both), with a number of laws pending in other jurisdictions.[2] Enacted laws have primarily focused on Burma; also targeted are Nigeria, Tibet, Cuba, Indonesia, Switzerland, and Northern Ireland, as well as poor foreign labor practices regardless of country.

## CONSTITUTIONAL ISSUES

The recent proliferation of state and local sanctions laws has raised questions regarding the constitutionality of such measures and prompted the filing of a federal court suit in April 1998 challenging Massachusetts' selective purchasing law targeted at Burma (Massachusetts Burma Law).[3] Three constitutional arguments are ordinarily made: (1) the laws burden commerce in violation of the Foreign Commerce Clause and, moreover, are not shielded by the market participant exception to the Commerce Clause; (2) they impermissibly interfere with the federal government's exclusive power to conduct foreign affairs; and (3) where the Congress or the President has acted, they are preempted by federal law.[4]

---

[2] Organization for International Investment, State and Municipal Sanctions Report, As of January 12, 2000 [http://www.ofii.org/issues/sanctions.html].

[3] The 1996 Massachusetts measure requires that a "restricted purchase list" be maintained containing the names of "all persons who currently do business with Burma (Myanmar)" and prohibits state entities from procuring goods or services from listed persons unless the procuring agency certifies that the procurement is "essential" and that compliance with the requirement "would eliminate the only bid or offer, or would result in inadequate competition" (Mass. Gen. Laws, ch. 7, §§ (22H(a)-(b), 22J). The procuring agency may award the contract to a covered person "only if there is no comparable low bid or offer by a person who is not on the restricted purchase list" (§ 22H(d)). A "comparable low bid or offer" is defined as "a responsive and responsible bid or offer which is no more than ten percent greater than the lowest bid or offer submitted for goods or a service" (§ 22G). Exemptions are also provided for news media, telecommunications operations, and certain medical supply businesses in Burma, and for state purchases of certain medical supplies (§§ 22H(e), 221).

[4] For legal background, see, *e.g.*, L. Henkin, *Foreign Affairs and the United States Constitution* (149-69 (2d ed. 1996) [hereafter cited as Henkin]; "Role of the States in Foreign Affairs," Part II of "Foreign Affairs Law at the End of the Century," 70 U. Colo. L. Rev. 1223 (1999); Price & Hannah, "The Constitutionality of United States State and Local Sanctions," 39 Harv. Int'l. L. J. 443 (1998) [hereafter cited as Price & Hannah]; Carvajal, "State and Local 'Free Burma' Laws: the Case for Sub-National Trade Sanctions," 29 Law & Pol'y Int'l Bus. 257 (1998)[hereafter cited as Carvajal]; Goldsmith, "Federal Courts, Foreign Affairs, and Federalism," 83 Va. L. Rev. 1617 (1997); Schmahmann & Finch, "The Unconstitutionality of State and Local Enactments in the United States Restricting Business Ties with Burma (Myanmar)," 30 Vand. J. Transnat'l L. 175 (1997) [hereafter cited as Schmahmann & Finch]; Bilder, "The Role of States and cities in Foreign Relations," 83 Am.J.Int'l L. 821 (1989) [hereafter cited as Bilder]. *See also* "Constitutionality of South African Divestment Statutes Enacted by State and Local Governments," 10 Op. Off. Legal Counsel 49 (1986) [hereafter cited as DOJ Opinion] {concluded that certain state divestment laws were constitutional).

## Foreign Commerce Clause

In granting Congress exclusive power to regulate interstate and foreign commerce (Art. I, § 8, cl. 3), the Constitution also impliedly prohibits states and localities from unreasonably burdening or discriminating against such commerce unless authorized by Congress to do so.[5] Opponents of state sanctions argue that such laws fall short of the Supreme Court test articulated in *Japan Line, Ltd. v. County of Los Angeles*, 441 U.S. 434 (1979), where the court required closer examination of a disputed measure when interference with foreign rather than interstate commerce is alleged. In striking down on Foreign Commerce Clause grounds a California state statute that applied an *ad valorem* property tax on foreign cargo containers, the Court stated that more demanding constitutional scrutiny was called for because of the need for the federal government to speak with one voice in U.S. foreign commercial relations, emphasizing that the failure to do so may cause the action of one sub-federal jurisdiction to invite retaliation against the nation as a whole. In subsequent state tax cases, however, the Supreme Court held that a state statute that "merely has foreign resonances, but does not implicate foreign affairs" does not violate the "one voice" principle, and that even a state statute that may make it more difficult for the federal government to speak in a solo international trade voice will be sustained if there is no clear indication that congress had intended to bar the state practice.[6] Because selective purchasing laws have a significant effect on U.S. foreign commerce and have not been condoned by congress, it is argued that they would fall under current Foreign Commerce Clause tests.[7] Others maintain, however, that the market participant doctrine exempts selective purchasing and investment laws form the Commerce Clause altogether.[8] First articulated by the Supreme Court in 1976 in *Hughes v. Alexandria Scrap Corp.*, 426 U.S. 794 (1976), the doctrine exempts those laws in which the state or local government acts as a buyer or seller of goods rather than as a regulator. At the same time, it is also argued that the market participant doctrine is inapplicable where the state attempts to affect behavior beyond the immediate market in which it is operating, that the doctrine does not immunize laws that may be challenged under other constitutional provisions, and that the Supreme Court has indicated that the doctrine may not even apply in Foreign Commerce Clause cases.[9]

---

[5] Kraft Gen. Foods v. Iowa Dept. of Revenue, 505 U.S. 71 (1992); South-Central Timber Dev., Inc. v. Wunnicke, 467 U.S. 82 (1984); Japan Line, Ltd. v. County of Los Angeles, 441 U.S. 424.

[6] Container Corp. of America v. Franchise Tax Board, 463 U.S. 159, 194 (1983), *reh'g denied*, 464 U.S. 909 (1983); Barclays Bank v. Franchise Tax Board of California, 510 U.S. 298 (1994). *See also* Wardair Canada Inc. v. Florida Dept. of Revenue, 477 U.S. 1 (1986).

[7] Price & Hannah, *supra* note 4, at 457-65; Schmahmann & Finch, *supra* note 4, at 189-91.

[8] E.g. Carvajal, *supra* note 4, at 270-74. Note also DOJ Opinion, *supra* note 4, at 53-59. *Trojan Technologies, Inc. v. Commw. of Pa.*, 916 F.2d 903, 909-913 (3d Cir. 1990), *cert. denied*, 510 U.S. 1212 (1991), applied the market participant doctrine to a state Buy America law.

[9] *See, e.g.*, South Central Timber Dev., Inc. v. Wunnicke, 467 U.S. at 99 (downstream effects); United Building & Construction Trades Council v. Mayor & Council of Camden, 465 U.S. 208 (1984)(no immunity from other constitutional challenges); Reeves, Inc. v. State, 447 U.S. at 437-38, n. 9 (application in Foreign Commerce Clause cases unclear). *See generally* Price & Hannah supra note 4, at 482-90; Schmahmann & Finch, supra note 4, at 191-95.

## Intrusion into Foreign Affairs

In *Zschernig v. Miller*, 389 U.S. 429 (1968), the Supreme Court struck down an Oregon law prohibiting non-resident aliens from inheriting property if they could not satisfy the state courts that they lived in a country that allowed U.S. nationals to inherit estates on a reciprocal basis and that payments to foreign heirs from the Oregon estate would not be confiscated.[10] While the federal government had not exercised its power in the area, the Court nonetheless found that the inquiries required by the state would result in "an intrusion by the State into the field of foreign affairs which the Constitution entrusts to the President and the Congress." While some have noted that *Zschernig* is unique in its finding of a dormant federal foreign affairs power and that its true parameters are unknown,[11] it is also argued that selective procurement laws are directed at influencing or scrutinizing foreign behavior in the manner that the *Zschernig* Court found objectionable.[12] It is also maintained that at least one state "Buy America" law has been struck down on foreign affairs grounds,[13] and that courts upholding restrictive procurement laws under such an attack have emphasized that the laws applied neutrally to all foreign products and thus did not require the assessment of a particular government's policies that might result in constitutional infirmity.[14]

## Federal Preemption

In exercising its delegated powers, Congress may, by virtue of the Supremacy Clause (Art. VI, cl. 2), preempt state and local laws that conflict with or are incompatible with federal legislation and thus limit the use of powers that a state or locality may exercise concurrently with Congress. Where Congress has not expressly preempted sate and local laws, two types of implied federal preemption may be found: *field preemption*, in which federal regulation is so pervasive that one can reasonably infer that states or localities have no role to play.[15] And *conflict preemp*tion, in which "compliance with both federal and state regulations is a physical impossibility,"[16] or where the state law, as described by the Supreme Court in *Hines v. Davidowitz*, 312 U.S. 52 (1941), "stands as an obstacle to

[10] The Court distinguished *Clark v. Allen*, 331 U.S. 503 (1947), a case upholding a similar California Statute, on the ground that the statute could be implemented through "a routine reading of foreign law" and did not require the particularized inquiries demanded by the Oregon law.

[11] Bilder, *supra* note 4, at 825-26; Henkin, *supra* note 4, at 162-62.

[12] E.g., Price & Hannah, *supra* note 4, at 457-65; Schmahmann & Finch, *supra* note 4, at 198-99.

[13] Bethlehem Steel Corp. v. Board of Commissioners of the Dept. of Water & Power of the City of Los Angeles, 276 Cal. App. 221 (1969).

[14] *See* K.S.B. Technical Sales Corp. v. North Jersey District Water Supply Comm'n, 381 A.2d 774 (N.J. 1977); Trojan Technologies, Inc. v. Commw. of Pa., 916 F.2d 903 (3d Cir. 1990), *cert. denied*, 501 U.S. 1212 (1991); and *generally* Hannah & Price, *supra* note 4, at 469-71. *See DOJ Opinion, supra* note 4, at 437-48, for an argument that the market participant doctrine should be generally applicable and thus shield state proprietary actions from *Zschernig*.

[15] *See, e.g.*, Wardair Canada Inc. v. Florida Dept. of Revenue, 477 U.S. at 6.

[16] Florida Lime & Avocado Growers, Inc. v. Paul, 373 U.S. 132, 142-43 (1963).

the accomplishment and execution of the full purposes and objectives of Congress."[17] In preemption cases involving foreign affairs, courts may well weigh the deference traditionally accorded areas subject to state and local regulation against the policy considerations implicated by the federal scheme affecting foreign affairs or commerce. In *Hines*, which invalidated a state alien registration statute in conflict with federal law, the Court reiterated the long-recognized constitutionally-based supremacy of federal authority in foreign affairs and made clear that any concurrent state power in the area must be "restricted to the narrowest of limits," distinguishing the states' limited authority with regard to aliens from their broadly-based power to tax. Depending on the nature of a state statute and the type of federal action taken to deal with a problematic foreign nation, opponents of a sanctions law are thus likely to argue that, in the absence of express preemption, a state law may conflict with federal laws and policies with respect to the activities and persons covered, or that there is reason to presume that Congress intended that all state and local measures targeting a particular country by preempted.[18] In response, it might be maintained, *inter alia*, that federal limitations on the exercise of proprietary powers to contract and invest must be expressly intended or must result from a highly pervasive federal scheme.[19] Moreover, state laws may arguable mandate consequences that differ from federal remedies or that do not exist on the federal level so long as the federal legislation or action involved does not constitute a "complex and interrelated federal scheme of law, remedy and administration."[20]

## Constitutional Challenge to the Massachusetts Burma Law

The absence of well-developed case law directly addressing sub-federal sanctions made the outcome of a constitutional challenge to state sanctions laws unclear. While various Supreme Court cases had examined aspects of such laws, none directly ruled on such a statute. Moreover, the few state cases scrutinizing such measures on constitutional grounds differed in result.[21] In *National Foreign Trade Council v. Baker*, 26 F.Supp.2d

[17] 312 U.S. 52, 67 (1941).

[18] Hannah & Price, *supra* note 4, at 472-78; Schmahmann & Finch, *supra* note 4, at 184-89.

[19] *See, e.g.*, DOJ Opinion, *supra* note 4, at 64-65.

[20] *See id.* at 65-66, citing Wisconsin Dept. of Industry, Labor, and Human Relations v. Gould, Inc., 475 U.S. 282, 286 (1986); Carvajal, *supra* note 4, at 261-65. Price & Hannah, *supra* note 4, at 476-78, argue that *Gould* supports preemption of certain state sanctions.

[21] *Compare, e.g., Bd. Of Trustees of Employees' Retirement System v. Mayor of Baltimore City*, 317 Md. 72, 562 A.2d 720 (Md. 1989), cert. denied, 493 U.S. 1093 (1990)(municipal ordinance requiring city pension funds to divest their holding in companies doing business in South Africa upheld in face of preemption, foreign affairs and Foreign Commerce Clause challenges) *with Springfield Rare Coin Galleries v. Johnson*, 115 Ill. 2d 221, 503 N.E. 2d 300, 307 (Ill. 1986)(state could not use its constitutional taxing power to exempt from state taxes coins and currencies issued by the United States or any foreign country except South Africa; creation of tax classification based on political and social policies of a single foreign nation impermissibly intruded into regulation of foreign affairs; "regulations which amount to embargoes or boycotts" found to be "outside the realm of permissible State activity").

287 (D.Mass.1998), the district court, relying in large part on *Zschernig,* held the Massachusetts Burma Law to be an unconstitutional infringement of the dormant federal foreign affairs power. The U.S. Court of Appeals for the First Circuit upheld the district court decision June 22, 1999, in the then-captioned *National Foreign Trade Council v. Natsios*, 181 F.3d 38, where it held that the law not only infringed upon the federal power to conduct foreign affairs, but also violated the Foreign Commerce Clause and was preempted by federal law. The Supreme Court agreed to review the decision in November 1999 and heard oral argument March 22, 2000. The United States filed an *amicus* brief urging affirmance of the First Circuit decision; congressional briefs were filed on both sides of the issue.

The Supreme Court held that the state law was preempted by federal Burma sanctions contained in the Foreign Operations Appropriations Act, 1997, § 570, 110 Stat. 3009-166, enacted by P.L. 104-208. Even though Congress had not expressly preempted state laws in the Act, the former would need to yield to the latter if preempted under field or conflict preemption principles. Applying the latter, the Court found that the state law served as "as obstacle to the accomplishment and execution of the full purposes and objectives of Congress," as it "undermines the intended purpose and 'natural effect' of at least three provisions of the federal Act, that its delegation of effective discretion to the President to control economic sanctions against Burma, its limitation of sanctions solely to United States persons and new investment, and its directive to proceed diplomatically in developing a comprehensive, multilateral strategy towards Burma." Citing earlier Supreme Court cases, the Court at the outset rejected the State's argument that the law could not be preempted because it involved the use of the State's spending power. The Court found the state law to lack the flexibility inherent in the federal statute, since the former had stringent application requirements, including no termination provision, while the latter authorized the President to lift federal measures in certain circumstances, allowed him to prohibit new investment based on findings that he would make, and provided national security waiver authority with regard to all sanctions imposed in the statute. Next, the court found the state law to exceed federal authorities by covering most state contracts, both foreign and domestic businesses, and firms that were already operating in Burma, whereas the federal law imposed sanctions solely on U.S. persons, authorized a prohibition on new investment only, and exempted purchase and sales contracts from any such ban. Finally, the state law had in practice impeded the President's ability to pursue the multilateral strategy envisioned in the federal act, the Court citing formal protests from U.S. trading partners, WTO complaints, and the distraction caused by the state law in discussions with foreign countries regarding the situation in Burma.

## FUTURE PROSPECTS

With regard to state or local sanctions deemed to be preempted by federal law, Congress could choose expressly to authorize such measures in new legislation.[22] It is also possible that a sub-national sanctions law could be written in a way that does not conflict with a federal enactment. Where Congress has not authorized or imposed federal sanctions against a particular country, state or local measures may be challenged on dormant foreign affairs or Foreign Commerce Clause grounds, given that the *Crosby* case did not address, and thus did not foreclose or limit the use of, these constitutional arguments. At the same time, questions remain as to the outcome of these arguments in a particular case – among them, whether legislative silence would be construed as implied authorization of a state sanctions law or, alternatively, as a manifestation of an overriding federal policy that a particular country not be subject to restrictive U.S. measures.

[22] On July 11, 2000, a federal court in Miami issued a permanent injunction against a Miami-Dade county ordinance requiring persons and firms wishing to do business with the country to sign an affidavit that they had not had dealings with Cuba. "Federal judge issues injunction barring Cuba ordinance," Associated Press, July 11, 2000, *available in* LEXIS, News Library, Curnws File. The ordinance had been preliminarily enjoined May 16. Miami Light Project v. Miami-Dada County, 97 F.Supp.2d 1174 (S.D. Fla. 2000).

# State Technology Development Strategies: The Role of High Tech Clusters

*Wendy H. Schacht*

## Introduction

There has been increasing congressional interest in efforts across the country to generate expanded regional economic growth through technological development and the creation of new firms.[1] Concurrently, and often in conjunction with on-going federal programs,[2] state activities to promote an environment conducive to technological innovation have expanded, typically focusing on the development of concentrations of high tech firms in specific localities. This report provides a framework for exploring the feasibility of generating such high tech clusters in states where they currently do not exist or are not easily identifiable. The information contained in these pages may be used to provide a common frame of reference for key decision-makers as they examine the possibility of creating clusters. The reasons for such actions are presented there, as are the characteristics typically associated with high growth entrepreneurial regions. A summary of the lessons learned by the successes and failures of other jurisdictions may provide a guide for additional discussion. Also offered are selected options for further consideration in designing next steps for the community.

---

[1] For a detailed discussion see: Congressional Research Service, *Technology Development: Federal-State Issues*, by Wendy H. Schacht, CRS Report 96-958, 22 November 1996.

[2] For additional information see: Congressional Research Service, *Industrial Competitiveness and Technological Advancement: Debate Over Government Policy*, CRS Issue Brief 91132, updated regularly.

## ECONOMIC GROWTH

Technological advancement is a key element of economic growth. Experts widely accept that technical progress is responsible for up to one-half the growth of the U.S. economy and is one principal driving force for increases in our standard of living. Historically, industrial expansion was based on the use of technology to exploit natural resources. Today, such growth tends to be founded on scientific discoveries and engineering knowledge (e.g., electronics, biomedical applications) and is even more dependent than before on the development and use of technology. Technological advance can drive the economy because it contributes to the creation of new goods and services, new industries, new jobs, and new capital. It can expand the range of services offered and extend the geographic distribution of those services. The application of technology also can contribute to the resolution of those national problems that are amenable to technological solutions.

Technological progress is achieved through innovation, the process that provides new and improved products, manufacturing processes, and services. It is an activity that may involve, among other things, idea origination, research, development, engineering commercialization, and diffusion throughout the marketplace. A concept can become an innovation without evolving through those separate steps. An invention becomes an innovation when it has been integrated into the economy such that the knowledge created is applied in production to increase productivity and quality, or results in a new or improved product or service that can be sold in the marketplace. It is only then that a significant stimulus to economic growth occurs.

Entrepreneurial firms often play an important role in technological advancement and economic growth. It usually is through these companies that the results of research and development are commercialized and brought to the marketplace. Thus, the current interest in creating an environment to facilitate the development of indigenous talent and to attract outside players. While the manufacturing facilities of high technology companies can bring an infusion of new jobs to a region, studies have shown that branch plants do not provide much additional high technology development.[3] Such businesses tend to move when it is cheaper to manufacture elsewhere even though they utilize a skilled workforce. In contrast, the R&D facilities of high tech companies generate higher value added jobs. It might be possible to devise mechanisms to use the location of a production plant to stimulate involvement of the R&D sectors of the relevant corporation. However, concentrating on branch plants poses problems in the "[t]he stifling effects of a branch plant economy on entrepreneurship are great and cannot easily be overcome by policies to locate government research facilities in backward regions in the hope of generating spin-offs."[4]

---

[3] Amy Glasmeier, "High-tech Policy, High-tech Realities: The Spatial Distribution of High-tech Industry in America," in *Growth Policy in the age of High Technology, The Role of Regions and States*, ed. Jurgen Schmandt and Robert Wilson. (Boston: Unwin Hyman, 1990), 92.

[4] Edward J. Malecki, "Entrepreneurs, Networks, and Economic Development: A Review of Recent Research," *Advances in Entrepreneurship, Firm Emergence and Growth 3* (1997): 60.

Economic benefits remain within a region through the creation of new firms.[5] These companies create wealth through value added jobs that are long term and require highly skilled employees that generate additional income, spending, and growth, as well as more jobs. The regions that display an active entrepreneurial environment embody distinctive, and similar, characteristics. These areas typically have a knowledge source, generally a university that can provide a supply of ideas and employees, and on-going R&D. Venture capital is available as is skilled labor. There are clusters (or agglomerations) of similar entrepreneurial firms and opportunities for generating new businesses through science parks or incubators. Good transportation and a high standard of living are also complementary to entrepreneurial activity.

A critical mass of high technology companies is necessary to sustain indigenous economic growth. "An existing agglomeration [cluster] of firms in similar or related sectors is a principal determinant of both birth rates and the distribution of small technology-based firms."[6] Clusters are groups of interrelated companies and institutions (including suppliers, service providers, universities, and trade associations, etc.) located in a specific area that cooperate as well as compete.[7] As such, clusters provide the opportunity for on-going innovation to meet new demands for products and processes generated by the dynamic relationships among the players. Diversity within the types and sizes of businesses contributes to a good entrepreneurial environment.[8] A varied, educated, and skilled workforce also contributes to the technological advancement in and around the cluster.

Clusters are important not primarily because of production but because of the opportunities for knowledge spillovers.[9] "[I]nnovative activity is more likely to occur within close geographic proximity to the source of...knowledge, be it a university research laboratory, the research and development department of a corporation, or exposure to the knowledge embodied in a skilled worker,"[10] Innovation tends to cluster around industries where knowledge plays an important role[11] as evidenced by the biotechnology, computer, advanced materials, and telecommunications sectors, among others.

---

[5] Edward J. Malecki, "Technological Innovation and Paths to Regional Economic Growth," in *Growth Policy, 99.*

[6] Patricia M. Flynn, "Technology Life Cycles and State Economic Development Strategies," *Federal Reserve Bank of Boston, New England Economic Review*, May/June 1994, 24.

[7] Michael E. Porter, "Clusters and competition: New Agendas for Companies, Governments, and Institutions," *Harvard Business School, Division of Research Working Paper*, Sept. 1997 (revised 25 March 1998), 1.

[8] Malecki, *Entrepreneurs*, 68.

[9] David B. Audretsch and Maryann P. Feldman, "R&D Spillovers and the Geography of Innovation and Production," *American Economic Review*, June 1996, 631.

[10] Ibid., 638.

[11] Ibid.. 635. 637.

## LESSONS FROM THE PAST

In the quest for regional growth, state economic development strategies are based upon expansion of indigenous innovation and adaptation of technology in the private sector. Efforts are focused on the creation of high technology firms and the use of advanced technologies in the traditional manufacturing and service sectors. States are attempting to fashion an entrepreneurial climate by undertaking a variety of programs to assist existing technology-related businesses, to promote the development of new companies, and to facilitate the application of technologies and techniques in all industries. These endeavors vary by state and often several approaches are supported simultaneously. What they all have in common, however, is the potential to generate a large number of new, high value added jobs.

The economic distress brought about by the decline of traditional industries in the 1970s and 1980s and the subsequent loss of thousands of jobs helped spur the formulation of many of today's state programs.[12] The conditions precipitated a shift away from state policies to promote "smokestack chasing" – attracting large manufacturing firms away from other areas – toward assistance to high technology companies in the areas of research, development, commercialization, technology transfer, and capital formation, among others. Many of these efforts have crystallized into state "industrial policies" under which particular businesses or industrial sectors are selected as the nexus of state investment endeavors.

The activist nature of these state ventures has a foundation in their responsibilities to promote the economic viability within their jurisdictions. State involvement initially developed based on the idea that these non-national governments must take action in areas where the private sector was unwilling to play a role. Thus, the government was not seen as replacing the business community in the decision-making process, but as filling a void left by inaction.[13] In filling this void, the states saw an opportunity to attract or develop high technology firms which contribute to the area's economic growth through high-wage employment; low environmental costs; high rates of expansion; long-term growth potential; clustering of other similar firms and suppliers; export orientation; and prestige.[14]

Over the years, planned, coordinated efforts have been undertaken by states and localities to facilitate technological advancement and generate economic growth. Several have been highly successful; others have failed. In order to provide a framework for decisions in a particular area, it might be helpful to analyze efforts by several other regions and identify activities which might parallel the current situation under discussion. The study of Austin, Texas; Cape Canaveral, Florida; Research Triangle Park, North

---

[12] Matthew I. Slavin and Sy Adler, "Legislative Constraints on Gubernatorial Capacity for State Industrial Policy: Evidence from Oregon's Regional Strategies Program," *Economic Development Quarterly*, August 1996, 226.

[13] Jonathan Rauch, "Stateside Strategizing," *National Journal*, 27 May 1989, 1296.

[14] Larry Dildine referenced in Keith Ihlanfeldt, "Ten Principles for State Tax Incentives," *Economic Development Quarterly*, November 1995, 344.

Carolina; Phoenix, Arizona; and Lowell, Massachusetts may offer insights into what activities might be appropriate to areas of the country with few existing or identified clusters. The focus of this section is on *early* efforts by several communities because of perceived parallels with the current situation in many regions.

Critical to local technology development is a strong technological infrastructure and an entrepreneurial network.[15] This presents opportunities for state and local governments in pursuit of their responsibilities to promote economic development. However, it is important to keep in mind that some argue government policies are limited in what they can do to create entrepreneurs. Policy does not create entrepreneurs but can encourage them to stay in a location. There is a general finding that "...due to the complexity of the firm formulation process, it is hard for policies to transform an environment adverse to entrepreneurial activities into a favorable [sic] one."[16] By identifying what worked in other areas, decision-makers can identify what resources their individual state or locality has to offer the entrepreneur and what might be done to augment this foundation.

The history of the Austin area provides an interesting study for decision-makers in regions with federal facilities. Several of the factors necessary for a strong technological infrastructure were already in place; others needed to be developed. Federal facilities played a role in generating the critical mass required for the effort in Austin to succeed. Bergstrom Air Force base employed a large number of trained individuals and placed government funds into the local economy. Balcones Research Park was created in the early 1940s when the federal government provided land to the University of Texas and funded research tied to World War II.[17] The federal government has continued to facilitate development in the area by on-going funding for R&D.

The contribution of a strong academic institution in generating entrepreneurship and technological development is underscored by the role of the University of Texas (UT) in the Austin area. The University has been the source for the development of numerous indigenous firms. Over half of the small and medium sized companies existing in the locality during 1986 were spun-off from UT. The potential for on-going interaction with the university was part of the decision for entrepreneurs to remain in Austin.[18] Tracor Corporation, a Fortune 500 company in the mid-1980s, exemplified the generation of new, entrepreneurial growth through a research university. Created by a UT graduate, over 16 companies had spun-out of the original firm, employing almost 5,500 people in 1985. These spin-offs also spawned additional new companies. This growth would not have occurred without the existence of the University of Texas.[19]

The depth of higher education within Texas also played an important role in the 1983 decision by the Microelectronics and Computer Technology Corporation (a joint R&D

---

[15] Malecki in *Growth Policy*, 99.

[16] E.J. Malecki and F. Todtling, "The New Flexible Economy: Shaping Regional and Local Institutions for Global Competition," in *Technological Change, Economic Development and Space*, ed. C.S. Bertuglia et al. (Berlin, Springer, 1995), 281.

[17] David V. Gibson and Raymond W. Smilor, "Creating and Sustaining the U.S. Technopolis," in *Growth Policy*, 392.

[18] Ibid., 388.

[19] Ibid.. 404.

venture supported by various companies) to locate in Austin. Between 1970 and the early 1980s, Texas undertook a planned program to improve the state university system and 800 new chairs were endowed at UT.[20] This was accompanied by local level promotion of technology development that resulted in various public-private initiatives. A study of the reasons for the location decision by the Microelectronics and Computer Technology Corporation identified as significant the coordinated and cooperative effort by academic, business and government (state and local) leaders to offer a wide range of incentives including support for education at the University of Texas and Texas A&M University.[21] Similarly, the primary reason given for the decision by SEMATECH (a consortium of semiconductor manufacturing firms) to locate in Austin was the "support and cooperation of state and local public and private agencies."[22] The Chamber of Commerce provided information to and support of high tech companies while local groups brought together key individuals and organizations in a strategic approach to meeting their goals.[23]

Efforts to develop viable high tech industrial expansion in Florida coalesced around the federal facilities in Cape Canaveral.[24] Large aerospace and defense contractors were able to induce high tech growth through the recruitment of skilled workers and the training of local employees. The state also made a commitment to the pursuit of technological advancement to ensure that the opportunities presented were not lost. The area's infrastructure, particularly transportation, was strengthened. Academic resources were considered inferior and a concerted effort was made to improve the system at all levels including pre-college through graduate school, as well as vocational education. Educational programs were designed to meet industry needs and state funding was provided for engineering and science programs in the universities and for community and vocational schools. By 1987, there were over 400 specialized academic research programs of interest to industry in the state.

Another region which focused on improvements in the educational establishment was Research Triangle Park, North Carolina. There are three research universities in the area including the University of North Carolina, North Carolina State University, and Duke University. In 1959, Research Triangle Park (RTP) was created as a university affiliated research campus. The objectives of the Park were the diversification of the economy, the augmentation of high value added jobs, and additional employment opportunities for university graduates.[25] Although the state provided no direct funding, it built the

---

[20] Jurgen Schmandt and Robert Wilson, eds., *Promoting High-Technology Industry, Initiatives and Policies for State Governments* (Boulder, Westview Press, 1987), 242.

[21] Raymond W. Smilor, George Kozmetsky, and David V. Gibson, eds., *Creating the Technopolis* (Cambridge, Ballinger, 1988), 174-175.

[22] Gibson and Smilor in *Growth Policy*, 385.

[23] Smilor, Kozmetsky, and Gibson, in *Creating*, 167.

[24] Discussion from Schmandt and Wilson, eds., in *Promoting*, 45-63.

[25] Michael I. Luger and Harvey A. Goldstein, *Technology in the Garden, Research Parks and Regional Economic Development* (Chapel Hill: University of North Carolina Press, 1991), 82.

necessary roads for the Park[26] and donated the land for the Research Triangle Institute.[27] The institute offers research and development staff and facilities to companies.

A planned attempt was made to develop high technology industry by attracting the R&D facilities of large, established companies.[28] The area developed slowly until IBM moved in and the National Institute of Environmental Health Science (National Institutes of Health) located in the Park partly as a result of political influence by the U.S. Secretary of Commerce Luther Hodges, the former governor of North Carolina, and then Governor Terry Sanford. Numerous other R&D organizations have set up facilities in the Park since that time. Among the reasons for the decision to relocate were the "prestige" of being associated with the Park; the ability to interact with professionals in other organizations; and access to entry level graduates for recruiting purposes.[29]

The ability for an area to develop a viable and prosperous research park is dependent on several factors, although all need not be present for success. An existing R&D infrastructure and on-going research activity is one potential element. The availability of local research universities, engineering schools, or medical schools also plays a role along with good air transportation as well as technical and businesses services. Leadership is important and should include representatives from the political, academic, and business communities.[30]

The focus on recruiting existing firms has resulted in slower growth for the Park as other areas across the nation have been successful in developing additional resources. Through the early 1990s, there were few efforts within Research Triangle Park to generate new, start-up, high-tech companies and it was often too costly for small firms to locate within its confines.[31] However, there were other efforts, outside of RTP, to facilitate new firm growth. The state concentrated on improving the educational system to mold indigenous scientific and technical talent and developed job training programs through an extensive number of community colleges to attract new industries.[32]

Educational opportunities also played a significant role in high tech development around Phoenix, Arizona. One 1987 study funded by the National Science Foundation found that 70% of microelectronics firms attributed their decision to locate in Phoenix to the proximity of Arizona State University.[33] The state had made a coordinated effort to strengthen and expand the undergraduate and graduate programs as well as its research capabilities. As a result, the engineering curriculum was augmented, centers of excellence were created, and facilities for continuing engineering education were established, as was a research park to foster industry-university cooperative activities.[34]

---

[26] Schmandt and Wilson, eds., in *Promoting*, 171.
[27] Ibid., 186.
[28] Ibid., 63.
[29] Luger and Goldstein, *Garden*, 85, 87.
[30] Ibid., 175.
[31] Ibid., 78.
[32] Ibid., 173, 188.
[33] Gibson and Smilor in *Growth Policy*, 388-389.
[34] Ibid.. 389-390.

Part of the success of Phoenix has been attributed to the mix and diversity of industry in the area. Relocation of high technology firms to the region was one factor in its economic growth. However, concerns were raised as to the reliance on branch plants.[35] In the early 1980s, the state made a clear statement of commitment to the expansion of local businesses and the encouragement of entrepreneurial start-up firms as part of its strategic plan.[36] High tech growth in the region has been due to the expansion of existing firms, relocation of national corporations, spin-offs, or new start-ups.[37] Firms are attracted to Phoenix, or decide to remain, because of the availability of a trained work force and on-going R&D.[38]

Other lessons might be learned from the experience of Lowell, Massachusetts. In the mid-1980s, Lowell had become a "high tech success" after having experienced economic decline with the deterioration of traditional manufacturing in the area.[39] This success was based on attracting one major computer company, Wang Laboratories, and the subsequent location of several other similar firms in the region. The factors which contributed to the growing economy were familiar: entrepreneurial and skilled workers; a local competitive advantage in high technology; public and private financial resources; and effective local leadership. However, this did not last. The economic decline in the United States and particularly in the Northeast, a regional banking crisis caused by too many risk loans to small and medium sized companies, the effects of development life-cycles in the computer industry, and an over-reliance on one industrial sector and on one firm, all combined to negate the prior economic growth. This situation highlights the importance of diversifying the industrial and employment base, and providing the skills necessary to support various sectors. Sustained growth requires on-going investment in R&D and innovation and the support of entrepreneurs in numerous types of businesses.

As discussed above, certain characteristics are found in entrepreneurial areas, including a knowledge source, on-going R&D, a skilled workforce, clusters of high tech firms, and good transportation. Commonalities associated with successful programs designed to encourage entrepreneurship include on-going leadership, either by state or local officials or representatives of the private sector. Strategic studies that identify the strengths and weaknesses of the area, increase the visibility of the effort, expand awareness of the process, and develop support are often important. The critical role of education cannot be ignored nor can the development of human resources through training.[40] Also present are research and development activities directed toward new products and processes. Promotion of entrepreneurship, often through incubator programs, aims at developing the critical mass necessary for innovative activity. Public-

---

[35] Smilor, Kozmetsky, and Gibson, *Creating*, 201.

[36] Peter K. Eisinger, *The Rise of the Entrepreneurial State* (Madison, University of Wisconsin Press, 1988), 238.

[37] Smilor, Kozmetsky, and Gibson, *Creating*, 190.

[38] Ibid., 192, 194.

[39] Discussion from Ross J. Gittell and Patricia M. Flynn, "The Lowell High-Tech Success Story: What Went Wrong?" *Federal Reserve Bank of Boston New England Economic Review*, March/April 1995, 57-68.

[40] Schmandt and Wilson, *Promoting*, 260-261.

private cooperation is also necessary for developing a commitment by all involved parties, particularly when such efforts tend to require patience.[41]

## Ideas for Consideration in Employing the High Tech Cluster Concept

It should be recognized that "the development of regional research and development and scientific complexes take long periods of time, and economic effects such as the generation of new local industries are highly unpredictable."[42] It might be helpful to states interested in using high tech clusters to stimulate economic growth to identify local resources including universities, technical and vocations colleges, industrial facilities, small businesses, federal institutions, and federal laboratories. Also of importance is information on research and development expenditures in the state. What is the percent of R&D as a portion of gross domestic product in the state? What is the role of federal funding for R&D in the area, what does the state finance in this area, and how much does industry spend? In addition, questions need to be answered as to where the educational system stands, particularly in the areas of science, technology, and engineering. What if the level of state support for education, higher education, and academic R&D? This material, as well as related economic, educational, scientific, and technical data particular to each state often can be obtained from the National Science Foundation or from state agencies.

A detailed guide for any community attempting to plan for an entrepreneurial environment is published by the Economic Development Administration of the Department of Commerce. Titled *Cluster-Based Economic Development: A Key to Regional Competitiveness*, this report furnishes a discussion of the specific steps that may be involved in an organized effort at the state and local level. In addition, if a pro-active approach is to be taken, certain ideas may need to be considered. Several are identified below.

### Cluster Development

- What industry clusters exist in the region, if any?
- What might be done to support/expand existing clusters?
- What clusters might be developed given resources in the area?
- What might be necessary to develop new clusters?
- Is there sufficient R&D/industry support for clusters?
- What are the characteristics of the state that might support clusters?

---

[41] Ibid., 261.

[42] Malecki in *Growth Policy*, 99.

## The Workforce

- What is the make-up of the existing workforce in the state?
- What are the current workforce needs of the state?
- What are the future needs of the state's workforce?
- How should be workforce be trained/educated?
- Who should train/educate the workforce?
- Who will pay for workforce training?

## Education

- What are the educational resources of area universities?
- What is the status of academic programming tied to high tech development?
- What new or expanded programs are needed to meet the demands of the cluster(s)?
- What type of vocational education is available?
- What vocational education programs are needed?
- Who will pay for expanded university and vocational education activities?

## Research and Development

- What are the R&D resources of any federal laboratories in the area?
- How can the resources of such federal laboratories be utilized?
- What existing federal R&D programs might be relevant?
- How can on-going federal programs be incorporated into state efforts?
- What is the role of any existing science parks?
- What are the R&D resources of the universities?
- What is the proper level of R&D in the universities?
- Who should pay for the proper level of R&D in universities?
- How best can knowledge spill-overs be captured in the state?

## Business Environment

- What are the benefits/costs of small business incubators in cluster development?
- How can venture capital be created or attracted to the state?
- How can a diversified industrial base be achieved?
- How can existing branch plants attract R&D facilities?
- How can indigenous entrepreneurs be encouraged?
- What are the high tech clusters?
- Is transportation sufficient to support high tech entrepreneurship?

Developing high tech clusters is one approach to creating increased economic growth through technological development and the generation of new firms. While this primarily may be a state function, much of what can be done depends on building upon federal programs, utilizing federal facilities, and leveraging federal funding for R&D and education. In addressing the issues, it should be noted that the experiences of other regions indicate that the development of public-private partnerships are critical to generating and taking advantage of the opportunities for economic growth. Representation from federal, state, and local governments as well as the business and academic communities can insure that all players are committed to the process and that unnecessary duplication of efforts does not occur. It has been shown that each sector needs to have a stake in the planning and implementation of any coordinated effort for it to be a success.

# CITIZEN INITIATIVE PROPOSALS APPEARING ON STATE BALLOTS, 1976-1992

*Lisa Oakley and Thomas H. Neale*

## INTRODUCTION

The direct democracy movement that arose out of Progressivism and Populism during the late 19th and early 20th centuries sought to counter contemporary political corruption and election fraud by promoting the use of three processes – recall, referendum, and initiative. The movement aimed at providing greater public involvement in the control over nominations to public office, voting procedures, and the legislative process itself.

Initiative, the topic of this analysis, is a legislative process through which voters propose laws or constitutional amendments through a process of petition and enact them through popular vote, independently of legislatures. It is an additional and direct way for voters to control legislative procedures and outcomes, beyond voting for issues or legislators at the polls.

The U.S. Constitution, in Article I, Section 1, vests "all legislative powers" in the Congress. This requirement established the United States Government as a representative democracy within a republican and federal framework, and the use of initiative on the Federal or national level is almost universally interpreted as precluded, absent, a constitutional amendment.[1]

Various forms of initiative and other forms of direct democracy have been established in a number of States, however, beginning as early as 1898, when South Dakota enacted statewide initiative procedures.[2] A number of States authorize direct democracy procedures on the local level as well. Thirty-two States and the District of

---

[1] U.S. Library of Congress. Congressional Research Service. *Initiative, Referendum and Recall by Citizen Petition*. CRS Report for Congress 93-590 A, by Thomas M. Durbin and M. Ann Wolfe. Washington, 1993, p. CRS-5.

[2] Cronin, Thomas E. *Direct Democracy: The Politics of Initiative, Referendum, and Recall*. Cambridge, MA, Harvard University Press, 1989. p. 51.

Columbia currently provide for one or more of the four direct democracy processes listed below. A requisite number of registered voters (requirements vary from State to State) must sign and present petitions to State authorities in each of these procedures before the corresponding initiative, referendum, or recall election can be scheduled. The four varieties of direct democracy procedures are:

- *Direct Initiative:* Qualifies a constitutional amendment or law for inclusion on the State ballot as it is written, where majority approval is necessary for passage.[3]
- *Indirect Initiative:* Refers a measure to the Sate legislature. If the legislature rejects the measure or fails to act, it is automatically included on the State ballot, where majority approval is necessary for passage. Some States authorize the legislature to submit an alternative measure.
- *Referendum:* Refers a measure previously enacted by the State legislature for inclusion on the State ballot for confirmation or reversal by majority vote.
- *Recall:* Requires a designated elected official to submit to a recall election, in which the official is retained or removed by majority vote.

Citizen initiative generally empowers voters to submit proposed legislation – and sometimes constitutional amendments – directly to the electorate for approval. There is a substantial variation among the States in the type of initiative they may have: some provide for statutes or constitutional amendments by citizen initiative; some provide both, either directly or indirectly. Others have mixed procedures, such as direct initiative for constitutional amendments, but indirect for statutes, while some States do just the opposite. In addition, most States prohibit initiatives on certain questions, most commonly revenue measures, appropriations, act affecting the judiciary, local or special legislation, and laws affecting public order, health, or safety. Of the four direct democracy processes cited above, direct initiative is arguably most independent of influence or control by State legislatures, as initiatives are generally not subject to veto by the governor or amendment or repeal by the legislature.

This report surveys citizen initiative activity for the years 1976 through 1992. It includes information about institutional details and election results for each State providing for citizen initiative: types of initiative available to voters in the State; date of adoption; petition requirements and voting rules; filing fees; date and summary descriptions of individual initiative items (including type); and election results for each measure in the period covered.

---

[3] A few States allow bonds or memorials to qualify for direct placement on the ballot. Some States have (or have had) supermajority requirements for passage of initiatives. See the State pages below.

# INITIATIVES APPEARING ON STATE BALLOTS, 1976-1992: A SUMMARY

Issues that qualified for placement on State ballots in this period covered 18 subjects, ranging from abortion to utility rates. Table 1 summarizes statistics for each subject, i.e., number, the number that passed, and respective passage rates of all initiatives for each of the 18 subjects. The table lists initiatives by subject, as indicated in the ballot titles.[4] Adjacent to the description of the initiative type is the abbreviation code used in the body of the Report.

**Table 1. Number of Initiatives by Type, 1976-1992**

| | | Passed | |
|---|---|---|---|
| **Issue** | **Total** | **Number** | **Rate** |
| Abortion | 12 | 3 | 25.0% |
| Beverage Containers, Recycling (bev) | 15 | 1 | 6.7% |
| Budgets, Spending, Taxes, Bonds (bud) | 134 | 55 | 41.0% |
| Campaign, Lobbying Laws (cam) | 10 | 8 | 80.0% |
| Consumer, Auto Insurance (con) | 11 | 2 | 18.2% |
| Crime and Punishment (cri) | 27 | 17 | 63.0% |
| Educational Standards, Operations (edu) | 11 | 2 | 18.2% |
| English as Official Language (eng) | 5 | 5 | 100.0% |
| Health Care Financing (hea) | 10 | 1 | 10.0% |
| Lottery, Gambling (lot) | 31 | 11 | 35.5% |
| Nuclear Weapons (nw) | 10 | 7 | 70.0% |
| Nuclear Power, Hazardous Waste (np) | 37 | 16 | 43.2% |
| Redistricting, Legislative Powers (red) | 20 | 11 | 55.0% |
| Sexuality and gender/AIDS (sex) | 8 | 2 | 25.0% |
| Term Limitations (ter) | 20 | 18 | 90.0% |
| Voting Rights, Registration, Elections (vot) | 15 | 10 | 66.7% |
| Utilities: Rates, Commissions (uti) | 16 | 7 | 43.7% |
| Other Issues (oth) | 103 | 40 | 38.8% |
| Total | 495 | 216 | 43.6% |

## Comparative Passage Rates by Issue Type

Initiatives to make English the Official Language had the highest passage rate – 100 percent – although there were only five such propositions. Term limits and campaign/lobbying propositions saw the next highest passage rates at 90 percent and 80

[4] Issue classification was determined through use of official voter information pamphlets, where available.

percent respectively. What appear to advisory Memorials to the Federal Government regarding nuclear weapons saw a passage rate of 70 percent. Crime propositions followed next with a rate of 63 percent. This classification included: drinking age and marijuana laws; handgun controls; victims' rights; obscenity statutes; and violent crime. Initiatives concerning violent crime or violent criminals enjoyed a higher passage rate than the group as a whole. Propositions dealing with redistricting, legislative sessions, recall, and restrictions on the size or powers of the legislatures passed at a rate of 55 percent. Ballot items dealing with construction of nuclear power plants and waste disposal passed at a rate of 43 percent. Proposals related to public finance or budgetary questions passed at a rate of 41 percent and included any initiative dealing with taxation or tax rates, government spending, and bonds; over one-fourth of the initiatives fell into this category. Abortion and sexuality and gender/AIDS initiatives had passage rates of 25 percent. Those concerning health care financing, consumer and auto insurance, and beverage containers or recycling enjoyed the lowest passage rates. The category "Other Issues" includes all other questions nor numerous enough to classify in their own category, or not obviously falling into any of the other 17. Regulation of milk prices, Sunday closing laws, safety belt laws, and labor rights are examples of these initiatives.

## Summary Statistics: 1904-1992

The rate of direct citizen activity, as measured by initiatives per year, nearly tripled in the 1976-1992 period when compared to the entire 1904-1975 period covered by Graham (1978). The passage rate for initiatives by petition has also increased: the rate at which initiatives passed in the 1976-1992 period was 43.6 percent, compared with the passage rate from the previous 1904-1975 period of 38.7 percent.

In the 1976-1992 period, citizens in 23 states petitioned 495 measures to State ballots, of which voters adopted 216 and rejected 279. A general breakdown of the passage and failure of initiatives and the number of States with initiative in this period are shown in table 2 below:

**Table 2. Initiatives Passed and Failed, 1976-1992**

| | Passed | Failed | Total | Passage Rate | No. of States |
|---|---|---|---|---|---|
| Constitutional Amendments | 86 | 108 | 194 | 44.3% | 16 |
| Statutes | 90 | 130 | 220 | 40.9% | 15 |
| Indirect Statutes | 31 | 39 | 70 | 44.3% | 8 |
| Memorials | 8 | 2 | 10 | 80.0% | 10 |
| Bonds | 1 | 0 | 1 | 100.0% | 1 |
| Total | 216 | 279 | 495 | 43.6% | |

Between 1904 and 1975, 1,172 measures were initiated by petition through direct and indirect processes; 453 were adopted by voters, and the remaining 719 were rejected.[5] Statistics for special initiative types in the1904-1975 period are shown in Table 3:

**Table 3. Initiatives Passed and Failed, 1904-1975**

| | Passed | Failed | Total | Passage Rate | No. of States |
|---|---|---|---|---|---|
| Constitutional amendments | 192 | 324 | 516 | 37.5% | 16 |
| Indirect const. amendments[6] | 9 | 0 | 9 | 100.0% | 2 |
| Statutes | 219 | 342 | 561 | 39.0% | 15 |
| Indirect statutes | 33 | 53 | 86 | 38.4% | 9 |
| Total | 453 | 719 | 1172 | 38.7% | |

The statistics differ between the two blocks of time, yet, the blocks of time are unequal. However, comparisons between initiative activity in the current 17-year period and the earlier period can be made if the larger 1904-1975 period is broken down into individual interval lengths which correspond closely to the period covered by this report. Four 18-year periods lie within the larger period; the following tables summarize activity in each of these 18-year blocks: 1904-1921, 1922-1939, 1940-1957, and 1958-1975. The tables show that the sue of citizen initiative increased during the 1904-1921 and 1922-1939 periods, then steadily declined throughout the next two periods, and finally rebounded to surpass the 1922-39 level during the current 1976-1992 period. In a mirror image of this trend, passage rates of citizen-initiated legislation fell from 40 percent in the first period to just under 34 percent between 1922 and 39, then increased in each of the subsequent two periods, but, again, have declined slightly in the current period from the fourth period rate. Thus, in purely statistical terms, as the volume of initiative activity increased between the periods examined, the corresponding rates of passage decreased. Table 4 summarizes activity during four 18-year intervals between 1904 and 1975. Figure 1 displays patterns between aggregate initiative use and passage rates.

[5] Some bills approved by voters in Oklahoma did not meet the requirement that the number of Yes votes must be at least as great as half the number voting in the entire election. While they may have had majority approval from those voting on the measure, these are counted as failed. This passage criterion changed in 1974.

[6] Seven indirect constitutional amendments were solely in North Dakota in 1918, before that State provided direct initiative for amendments. The other two were in Massachusetts.

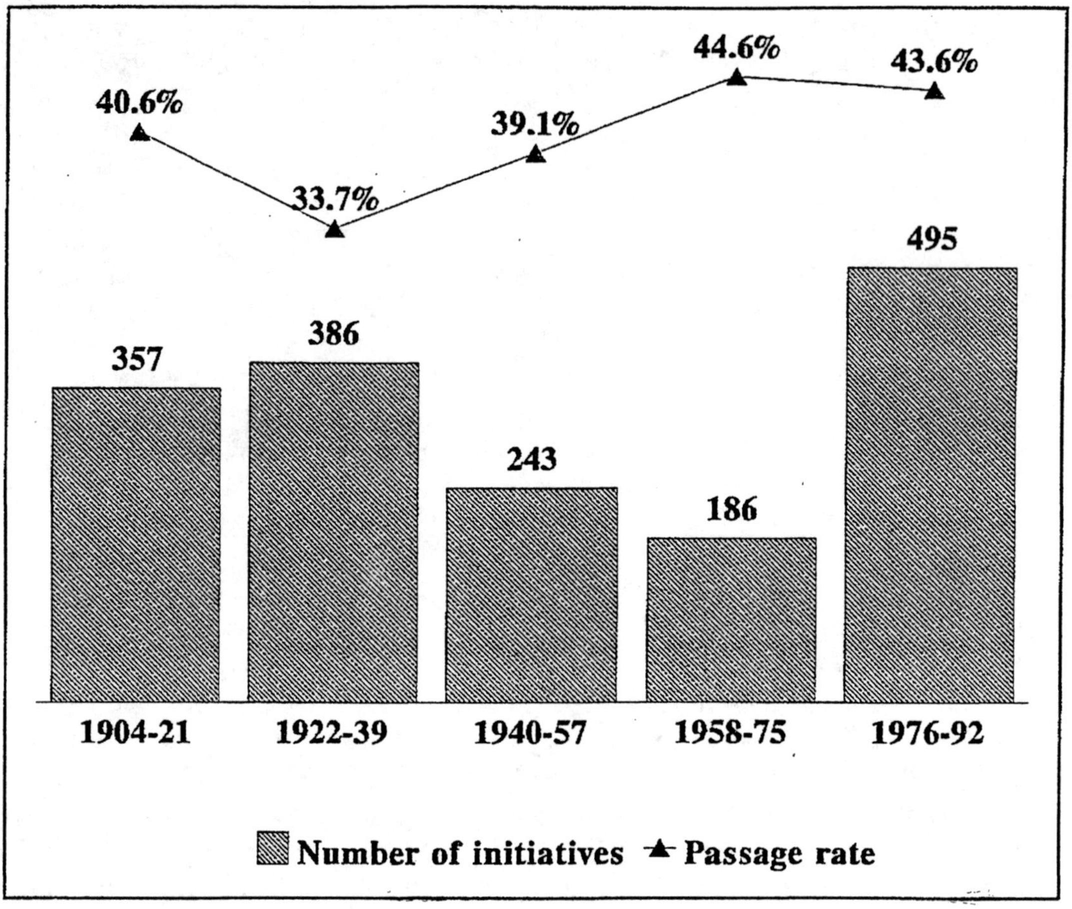


**Figure 1. Number of Initiatives and Passage Rate**

## Debate about Citizen Initiative

The arguments for and against an institution like citizen initiative in a representative democracy vary as widely as the topics the initiatives may cover.[7] Some of the most prominent criticisms raised *against* citizen initiative include: special interests can abuse citizen initiative; "big money" has a great advantage; voters may be deceived by signature gatherers on petition drives; initiatives are not always drafted in a manner consistent with the existing legal structure and often confuse voters; the court costs involved in determining the constitutionality of passed initiatives are too high; too many issues on the ballot may cause voter turnout to decline; minority rights may not be

[7] The arguments are not limited to those listed here. For a full discussion on direct democracy issues, see: Cronin, *Direct Democracy: The Politics of Initiative, Referendum and Recall.* These summary statements are taken from pp. 10-11, 207-221. For a summary of the past proposals of National Initiative, see pp. 163-184.

adequately protected; and legislatures are directly weakened. Prominent arguments *in favor of* citizen initiative have included: initiative will increase government responsiveness and enforce accountability; it provides an alternative route to legislation to counter special interest influence in the legislature; initiative fosters public debate on issues aligned with voter interests and increases voter participation; and initiative allows citizens to address issues otherwise avoided by legislators.

Limitations placed on the initiative process and requirements for use of the initiative vary by State; these are detailed by State in the pages immediately following.

**Table 4. Initiatives Passed and Failed in 18-year Blocks**

| | Passed | Failed | Total | Passage Rate | No. of States |
|---|---|---|---|---|---|
| **1904-1921:** | | | | | |
| Constitutional amendments | 62 | 98 | 160 | 38.8% | 13 |
| Indirect const. amendments | 7 | 0 | 7 | 100.0% | 2 |
| Statutes | 71 | 106 | 177 | 40.1% | 13 |
| Indirect statutes | 5 | 8 | 13 | 38.5% | 9 |
| Total | 145 | 212 | 357 | 40.6% | |
| **1922-1939:** | | | | | |
| Constitutional amendments | 54 | 125 | 179 | 30.2% | 13 |
| Indirect const. amendments | 1 | 0 | 1 | 100.0% | 1 |
| Statutes | 64 | 115 | 179 | 35.8% | 13 |
| Indirect statutes | 11 | 16 | 27 | 40.7% | 9 |
| Total | 130 | 256 | 386 | 33.7% | |
| **1940-1957:** | | | | | |
| Constitutional amendments | 43 | 56 | 99 | 43.4% | 13 |
| Statutes | 6 | 72 | 118 | 39.0% | 13 |
| Indirect statutes | 6 | 20 | 26 | 23.1% | 9 |
| Total | 95 | 148 | 243 | 39.1% | |
| **1958-1975:** | | | | | |
| Constitutional amendments | 33 | 45 | 78 | 42.3% | 16 |
| Indirect const. amendments | 1 | 0 | 1 | 100.0% | 1 |
| Statutes | 38 | 49 | 87 | 43.7% | 15 |
| Indirect statutes | 11 | 9 | 20 | 55.0% | 9 |
| Total | 83 | 103 | 186 | 44.6% | |

## CONCLUSION

This report surveys citizen initiative activity in the States for the period 1976-1992, including requirements for ballot placement and criteria for passage. It presents a historical overview of past activity and detailed descriptions of initiative measures in the most recent (1976-1992) period. It also compares the magnitude of activity and passage rates of initiative activity in the current 1976-1992 period to periods of comparable length beginning with the period of 1904-1921. In general, initiative use and passage rates are negatively related; but both the use and passage of initiatives have increased from the first period to the current one.

## ALASKA

### What May Be Initiated

Direct initiation of statutes has been available to voters since 1959, when Alaska entered the Union. Constitutional amendments may not be submitted to the ballot through the initiative process.

### Petition Requirement

Signatures of not less than ten percent of voter turnout in the previous general election must be secured to place a statutory initiative on the ballot. In addition, the signatures must be gathered from residents in at least two-thirds of the electoral districts. Petitioners have a period of one year in which to gather signatures. Petitions are filed with the lieutenant governor; a refundable $100 deposit must accompany the filing application.

### Passage Requirement

A majority of the votes cast on the proposal is required for adoption.

**Summary of Activity from 1976 to 1992:**

| | Passed | Failed | Total |
|---|---|---|---|
| Statutes | 7 | 8 | 15 |
| Memorial | 1 | 0 | 1 |
| Total | 8 | 8 | 16 |

## Sources

Office of the Alaska Secretary of State, Division of Elections, *Initiatives Appearing on the Ballot in Alaska,* 1960-1990; Inter-University Consortium for Political and Social Research, *Referenda and Primary Election Materials, Part 49: Referenda Elections for Alaska*, 1968-1988; U.S. Library of Congress. Congressional Research Service. *A Compilation of Statewide Initiative Proposals Appearing on Ballots Through 1976.* Typed Report, by Virginia Graham, Jan. 12, 1978. Washington, 1978. (hereinafter cited as: Graham, *Compilation of Initiative Proposals*); U.S. Library of Congress. Congressional Research Service. *Initiative, Referendum and Recall: a Resume of State Provisions*, by Thomas Durbin. CRS Report for congress 81-63A. Washington, 1981. (hereinafter cited as Durbin, *Initiative, Referendum and Recall*); U.S. Library of Congress. Congressional Research Service. *Initiative, Referendum and Recall by Citizen Petition*, by Thomas M. Durbin and M. Ann Wolfe. CRS Report for Congress 93-590A. Washington, 1993. (hereinafter cited as: Durbin and Wolfe, *Initiative, Referendum and Recall*).

# ARIZONA

## What May Be Initiated

Direct initiation of both constitutional amendments and statutes has been available to voters since 1912, when Arizona entered the Union.

## Petition Requirement

*Constitutional Amendments*: Signatures of registered voters equal to fifteen percent of the total votes cast for all candidates for Governor at the preceding gubernatorial election must be secured to place an initiative on the ballot.

*Statutes*: Ten percent of the same is required. Petitions must be filed with the Secretary of State at least four months prior to the election and signatures must be gathered within twenty-four months prior to the general election.

## Passage Requirement

A majority of the votes cast on the proposal is required for adoption of either constitutional amendments or statutes.

**Summary of Activity from 1976 to 1992**

| | Passed | Failed | Total |
|---|---|---|---|
| Const. Amendments | 4 | 6 | 10 |
| Statutes | 4 | 9 | 13 |
| Total | 8 | 15 | 23 |

## Sources

Office of the Arizona Secretary of State, *Official Canvass of Votes*, 1976-1922; Secretary of State, *Publicity Pamphlet*, 1976-1992; Inter-University Consortium for Political and Social Research, *Referenda and Primary Election Materials, Part 38*: *Referenda Elections for Arizona*, 1968-1988; Graham, *Compilation of Statewide Proposals*; Durbin, *Initiative, Referendum and Recall*; Durbin and Wolfe, *Initiative, Referendum and Recall.*

# ARKANSAS

## What May Be Initiated

Direct initiation of both constitutional amendments and statutes has been available to voters since 1910.

## Petition Requirement

*Constitutional Amendments*: Signatures of registered voters equal to ten percent of the total number of votes cast for the office of Governor in the last general election must be gathered to place a constitutional amendment to the ballot. In addition, the signatures can be no less than five percent of the total county vote for the office of governor in at least fifteen counties.

*Statutes*: Signatures of registered voters equal to eight percent of the total number of votes cast for the office of Governor in the last general election must be gathered to place a statute on the ballot. In addition, the signatures can be no less than four percent of the total county vote for the office of governor in at least fifteen counties. All petitions are filed with the Secretary of State at least four months prior to the election.

## Passage Requirement

A majority of the votes cast on the proposal is required for adoption of either constitutional amendments or statutes.

**Summary of Activity from 1976 to 1992:**

| | Passed | Failed | Total |
|---|---|---|---|
| Const. amendments | 4 | 8 | 12 |
| Statutes[8] | 2 | 1 | 3 |
| Total | 6 | 9 | 15 |

## Source

Office of the Arkansas Secretary of State, *Proposed Constitutional Amendments, Initiatives and Referenda*, 1960-1992, compiled by W.J. "Bill" McCuen; Inter-University Consortium for Political and Social Research, *Referenda and Primary Election Materials, Part 24: Referenda Elections for Arkansas*, 1968-1988; Graham, *Compilation of Statewide Proposals*; Durbin, *Initiative, Referendum and Recall*; Durbin and Wolfe, *Initiative, Referendum and Recall.*

# CALIFORNIA

## What May Be Initiated

Direct initiation of both constitutional amendments and statutes have been available to voters since 1912. Indirect initiation of statutes was abolished in 1966.

## Petition Requirement

*Constitutional Amendments*: Signatures of registered voters equal in number to at least eight percent of the total vote case for the office of Governor at the preceding gubernatorial election are required to place a constitutional amendment on the ballot.

*Statutes*: Signatures from five percent of the same are required to place a statutory initiative on the ballot. Petitions must be filed with the Secretary of State; a limit on the circulation period of one hundred and fifty (150) days applies. A refundable $200 deposit must accompany the filing application. The initiative cannot be submitted to voters for at least one hundred and thirty-one (131) days after it qualifies, and the Governor may call a special election for the initiative.

[8] This total does not include three amendment initiatives which were removed from the ballot in this period: no 63 in 1982, no. 65 in 1984, and no. 4 in 1990.

## Passage Requirement

A majority of the votes cast on the proposal is required for adoption of either constitutional amendments or statutes.

**Summary of Activity from 1976 to 1992:**

| | Passed | Failed | Total |
|---|---|---|---|
| Const. amendments | 13 | 16 | 29 |
| Statutes[9] | 18 | 28 | 46 |
| Memorials | 1 | 0 | 1 |
| Bonds | 1 | 0 | 1 |
| Total | 33 | 44 | 77 |

## Source

Office of the California Secretary of State, *Election Returns*, Sacramento, California, 1986-1992; Office of the Secretary of State, *A Study of Ballot Measures: 1884-1986*, Sacramento, California; California Commission on Campaign Finance, *Democracy by Initiative: Shaping California's Fourth Branch of Government*, Los Angeles: Center for Responsive Government, 1992; Inter-University Consortium for Political and Social Research, *Referenda and Primary Election Materials, Part 46*: *Referenda Elections for California*, 1968-1988; Graham, *Compilation of Statewide Proposals*; Durbin, *Initiative, Referendum and Recall*; Durbin and Wolfe, *Initiative, Referendum and Recall.*

# COLORADO

## What May Be Initiated

Direct initiation of both constitutional amendments and statutes has been available to voters since 1910.

## Petition Requirement

Signatures of registered voters equal to five percent of the voter turnout at the previous election for all candidates for the office of Secretary of Sate must be secured to place either a constitutional amendment or a statute on the ballot.[10] Petitions are filed

[9] This total does not include initiated statute no. 35, which was removed from the ballot in 1984.

[10] Prior to December 19, 1980, the signature requirement was eight percent of the turnout at the previous election for all candidates in the race for Secretary of State. See Colorado Constitution, Art.V, Sec. 2.

with the Secretary of State at least three months before the election; a limit of six months on the petition circulation period applies.

## Passage Requirement

A majority of the votes cast on the proposal is required for adoption of either constitutional amendments or statutes.

**Summary of Activity from 1976 to 1992:**

| | Passed | Failed | Total |
|---|---|---|---|
| Const. amendments | 24 | 17 | 41 |
| Statutes | 2 | 7 | 9 |
| Memorial | 0 | 1 | 1 |
| Total | 26 | 25 | 51 |

## Source

Office of the Colorado Secretary of State, *Election Returns*, 1976-1992; Inter-University Consortium for Political and Social Research, *Referenda and Primary Election Materials, Part 39: Referenda Elections for Colorado*, 1968-1988; Graham, *Compilation of Statewide Proposals*; Durbin, *Initiative, Referendum and Recall*; Durbin and Wolfe, *Initiative, Referendum and Recall.*

# FLORIDA

## What May Be Initiated

Direct initiation of constitutional amendments has been available to voters since 1968. Statutes may not be submitted to the ballot through the initiative process.

## Petition Requirement

Signatures of registered voters equal to eight percent of the votes cast in the preceding general election from at least one half of the congressional districts in the State are required to place a constitutional amendment on the ballot. The number of signatures must also be not less than eight percent of the total number of votes cast in the preceding general election. Petitions are filed with the Secretary of State, and signatures are valid for a period of four years. Initiatives are placed on a general ballot at least ninety days after certification by the Secretary of State.

### Passage Requirement

A majority of the votes cast on the proposal is required for adoption.

**Summary of Activity from 1976 to 1992:**

| | Passed | Failed | Total |
|---|---|---|---|
| Const. amendments | 5 | 3 | 8 |

### Source

Office of the Florida Secretary of State, *Proposed Constitutional Amendments on Ballot*, 1976-1992; Office of the Secretary of State, *Election Returns*, 1976-1992; Inter-University Consortium for Political and social Research, *Referenda and Primary Election Materials, Part 25: Referenda Elections for Florida*, 1968-1988; Graham, *Compilation of Statewide Proposals*; Durbin, *Initiative, Referendum and Recall*; Durbin and Wolfe, *Initiative, Referendum and Recall.*

## IDAHO

### What May Be Initiated

Direct initiation of statutes has been available to voters since 1912. Constitutional amendments may not be submitted to the ballot through the initiative process.

### Petition Requirement

Signatures of registered voters equal to not less than ten percent of the aggregate vote case for Governor at the last gubernatorial election are required to place a statute on the ballot. Petitions must be filed with the Secretary of State four months before the election.

### Passage Requirement

Initiated statutes must receive a number of yes votes at least as great as the majority of votes cast in the gubernatorial contest in the same election.

**Summary of Activity from 1976 to 1992:**

| | Passed | Failed | Total |
|---|---|---|---|
| Statutes | 5 | 2 | 7 |

## Source

Office of the Idaho Secretary of State, *Abstract of Votes*, 1978-1982; Office of the Secretary of State, *Voter's Pamphlet*, 1978-1992; Inter-University Consortium for Political and Social Research, *Referenda and Primary Election Materials, Part 40: Referenda Elections for Idaho*, 1968-1988; Graham, *Compilation of Statewide Proposals*; Durbin, *Initiative, Referendum and Recall*; Durbin and Wolfe, *Initiative, Referendum and Recall.*

# ILLINOIS

## What May Be Initiated

Direct initiation of constitutional amendments has been available to voters since 1970. Statutes may not be submitted to the ballot through the initiative process. "Questions of Public Policy" may also be submitted to voters through a process of petition, but these measures are advisory and are treated as referenda. On public policy question on the subject of tax and spending limitations passed in 1978.

## Petition Requirement

Signatures of registered voters equal in number to at least eight percent of the total vote cast for Governor in the previous gubernatorial election are required to place a proposal on the ballot. Petitions are filed with the Secretary of State at least six months before the election, and petitions may be circulated for no more than 24 months prior to the general election.

## Passage Requirement

Affirmative votes from three-fifths of those voting on the proposal or a majority of those voting in the election is sufficient to pass a proposition.

**Summary of Activity from 1976 to 1992:**

| | Passed | Failed | Total |
|---|---|---|---|
| Const. amendments | 1 | 0 | 1 |

## Source

Illinois State Board of Elections, *Official Vote Cast at the General Election November 4, 1980*, pp. 22-23; similar voting records, 1976-1992; Inter-University Consortium for Political and Social Research, *Referenda and Primary Election Materials, Part 11: Referenda Elections for Illinois*, 1968-1988; Graham, *Compilation of Statewide Proposals*; Durbin, *Initiative, Referendum and Recall*; Durbin and Wolfe, *Initiative, Referendum and Recall.*

# MAINE

## What May Be Initiated

Indirect initiation of statutes through the legislature has been available to voters since 1908. Constitutional amendments may not be submitted to the ballot through the initiative process.

## Petition Requirement

Signatures equal to at least ten percent of the total votes cast for Governor in the preceding gubernatorial election are required to place a statute on the ballot. Petitions are filed with the Secretary of State by the 50th day after the legislatures convenes its first session, or by the 25th day after the legislature convenes its second session. Signatures older than one year are not valid.

## Passage Requirement

A majority of the votes cast in favor of the proposal is required for passage. The legislature may propose an alternative measure to voters; if neither receives a majority, yet on e receives a number of yes votes at least as great as one-third of the total cast on both measures, then this initiative is placed before the voters in a statewide election to be held not less than 60 days after the first vote.

**Summary of Activity from 1976 to 1992:**

| | Passed | Failed | Total |
|---|---|---|---|
| Indirect statutes[11] | 7 | 7 | 14 |
| Memorial | 1 | 0 | 1 |
| Total | 8 | 7 | 15 |

## Source

Office of the Maine Secretary of State, *An Election History of Initiatives*, 1971-91; Office of the Secretary of State, Voter Information Pamphlets, 1971-91; Inter-University Consortium for Political and Social Research, *Referenda and Primary Election Materials, Part 2: Referenda Elections for Maine*, 1968-1988; Graham, *Compilation of Statewide Proposals*; Durbin, *Initiative, Referendum and Recall*; Durbin and Wolfe, *Initiative, Referendum and Recall.*

# MASSACHUSETTS

## What May Be Initiated

Direct initiation of both constitutional amendments and statutes through the legislature (General Court) has been available to voters since 1918. The General court may submit to the people a legislative alternative to the measure.

## Petition Requirement

The proposed measure cannot be the same as any other that has appeared in the two preceding biennial elections. Signatures of registered voters equal in number to not less than three percent of the total votes cast for Governor in the preceding biennial State election are required to place either a constitutional or statutory measure on the ballot. No more than one-fourth of all signatures may come from a single county. Petitions for both constitutional amendments and indirect statutes are signed by ten registered voters as sponsors and are filed with the Secretary of State not earlier than the first Wednesday or September before the assembling of the General Court into which they will be introduced. The remainder of the signatures can be filed no later than the first Wednesday in the following December. If the legislature has not passed an initiated statute by the first Wednesday in May, petitioners must file a supplementary petition for an amended version of the measure with signatures equal in number to one-half of one

[11] In 1985, the legislature placed an alternative to the initiated proposal on the ballot; this was rejected and not counted here.

percent of the total votes cast in the previous gubernatorial election to place the measure on the ballot.

## Passage Requirement

*In the General Court:* One-fourth of all members elected to the General Court must approve the measure for it to be placed on the ballot in the next election; three-fourths of the legislators voting on the measure may amend it. The legislature may also present the voters with a legislative substitute; in the case of a constitutional amendment, it must be approved by a majority of legislators voting thereon in two succeeding joint sessions.

*At the Polls:* A majority of the votes cast on the original measure, an amended version, or a legislative substitute is required for passage; this number must be as great as 30 percent of the total votes cast in the election.

**Summary of Activity from 1976 to 1992:**

| | Passed | Failed | Total |
|---|---|---|---|
| Statutes[12] | 8 | 13 | 21 |

## Source

Office of the Secretary of the Commonwealth, *Election Returns*, 1976-1992; Office of the Secretary of the Commonwealth, *Massachusetts Information for Voters*, 1976-1992; Inter-University Consortium for Political and Social Research, *Referenda and Primary Election Materials, Part 3*: *Referenda Elections for Massachusetts*, 1968-1999; Graham, *Compilation of Statewide Proposals*; Durbin, *Initiative, Referendum and Recall*; Durbin and Wolfe, *Initiative, Referendum and Recall.*

# MICHIGAN

## What May Be Initiated

Direct initiation of constitutional amendments and indirect initiation of statutes through the legislature has been available to voters since 1913.

[12] No constitutional amendments were submitted to the ballot by voters in this period. All passing Statutes cleared the 30% of total turnout requirement.

## Petition Requirement

*Constitutional Amendments*: Signatures of registered voters equal in number to at least ten percent of the total votes cast for all candidates for Governor in the last gubernatorial election are required to place a constitutional amendment on the ballot.

*Statutes*: Signatures of the same equal in number to at least eight percent of the same must sign the petition submitting the statute to the legislature. Petitions for constitutional amendments must be submitted to the Secretary of State 120 days before the election at which it will be voted upon; petitions for statutes must be submitted ten days before the start of the legislative session.

## Passage Requirement

*Constitutional Amendments:* A majority of the votes cast on the proposal is sufficient for adoption of constitutional amendments.

*Indirect Statutes:* The legislature has 40 days to enact or reject a statutory proposal. In the event it is rejects, they may propose a substitute on the same subject, both of which will appear on the ballot submitted to the voters. A majority of the votes cast on the proposal at the polls is sufficient for adoption of the statute.

**Summary of Activity from 1976 to 1992:**

| | Passed | Failed | Total |
|---|---|---|---|
| Const. amendments | 4 | 10 | 14 |
| Statutes[13] | 3 | 2 | 5 |
| Memorial | 1 | 0 | 1 |
| Total | 8 | 12 | 20 |

## Source

Office of the Michigan Secretary of State, *How an Issue Becomes a Ballot Proposal,* August 1990; Office of the Secretary of State, Election Returns, 1992; Inter-University Consortium for Political and Social Research, *Referenda and Primary Election Materials, Part 13: Referenda Elections for Michigan*, 1968-1988; Graham, *Compilation of Statewide Proposals*; Durbin, *Initiative, Referendum and Recall*; Durbin and Wolfe, *Initiative, Referendum and Recall.*

[13] An indirect initiative approved by the legislature (topic: public funding of abortion) was submitted to a referendum in 1988. It does not appear here because the indirect initiative was not submitted to popular vote and referenda are not covered in this report.

# MISSISSIPPI

## What May Be Initiated

Direct initiation of constitutional amendments has been available to voters since 1992. Statutes may not be directly or indirectly initiated.

## Petition Requirement

Signatures of registered voters equal in number to not less than 12 percent of the votes cast for Governor at the preceding gubernatorial election are required to place a constitutional amendment on the ballot. Signatures must be evenly distributed throughout the five congressional districts. Petitions are filed with the Secretary of State not less than 90 days before the first day of the legislative session to which it will be submitted. Signatures must be gathered within a 12-month period, with a filing fee of $500 required. One public hearing on the proposal is required to be held in each congressional district.

## Passage Requirement

For an initiative not challenged with a legislative alternative to be adopted (it may have been amended by the legislature), a majority of the votes cast on the proposal as well as 40 percent of the total votes cast at the election is required. If there is a legislative alternative, voters are asked to choose between the citizen and legislative alternatives or reject both.

## Summary of Activity from 1976 to 1992:

Mississippi recently adopted Citizen Initiative in 1992; no initiatives have appeared on the ballot to date.

## Source

Dick Molpus, Mississippi Secretary of State, *Constitutional Initiative in Mississippi: A Citizen's Guide*, September 1993.

# MISSOURI

## What May Be Initiated

Direct initiation of both constitutional amendments and statutes has been available to voters since 1908.

## Petition Requirement

*Constitutional Amendments*: Signatures of registered voters numbering not less than eight percent of the votes cast for Governor at the preceding gubernatorial election are required to place a constitutional amendment on the ballot. Signatures must be eight percent in number from two-thirds of the Congressional districts as well.

*Statutes*: Signatures from five percent of the same are required to place statutory initiatives on the ballot. Petitions are filed with the Secretary of State not less than four months before the election.

## Passage Requirement

A majority of the votes cast for the proposal is required for adoption.

**Summary of Activity from 1976 to 1992:**

| | Passed | Failed | Total |
|---|---|---|---|
| Const. amendments | 6 | 5 | 11 |
| Statutes | 3 | 3 | 6 |
| Total | 9 | 8 | 17 |

## Source

Office of the Missouri Secretary of State, *General Election Returns*, 1990-1992; Office of the Secretary of State, *Official Ballot of Missouri*, 1992; Office of the Secretary of State, *Constitutional Initiatives in Missouri*, 1936-1988, and *The Statutory Initiative in Missouri*, 1922-1984; Inter-University Consortium for Political and Social Research, *Referenda and Primary Election Materials, Part 19: Referenda Elections for Missouri*, 1968-1988; Graham, *Compilation of Statewide Proposals*; Durbin, *Initiative, Referendum and Recall*; Durbin and Wolfe, *Initiative, Referendum and Recall.*

# Montana

## What May Be Initiated

Direct initiation of statutes was adopted in Montana in 1906; direct initiation of constitutional amendments has been available to voters since 1972.

## Petition Requirement

*Constitutional Amendments*: Signatures of a number of registered voters not less than ten percent of the total number registered and also in at least two-fifths of the legislative districts are required to place a constitutional amendment on the ballot.

*Statutes*: Signatures from five percent of the electors in at least one-third of the legislative districts are required to place a statutory initiative on the ballot. Petitions must be filed with the Secretary of State at least three months before the election.

## Passage Requirement

A majority of the votes cast in favor of the proposal is required for adoption.

**Summary of Activity from 1976 to 1992:**

| | Passed | Failed | Total |
|---|---|---|---|
| Const. amendments | 2 | 5 | 7 |
| Statutes | 11 | 9 | 20 |
| Memorial | 1 | 0 | 1 |
| Total | 14 | 14 | 28 |

## Source

Office of the Montana Secretary of State, Report of the Official Canvass of the Vote Cast, 1976-1992; Inter-University Consortium for Political and Social Research, Referenda and Primary Election Materials, Part 41: Referenda Elections for Montana, 1968-1988; Graham, Compilation of Statewide Proposals; Durbin, Initiative, Referendum and Recall: Durbin and Wolfe. Initiative. Referendum and Recall.

# NEBRASKA

## What May Be Initiated

Direct initiation of both constitutional amendments and statutes has been available to voters since 1912.

## Petition Requirement

*Constitutional Amendments*: Signatures from a number of registered voters equal to at least ten percent of the total number voting in the previous gubernatorial election are required to place a constitutional amendment on the ballot. The same signatures must be so distributed as to include five percent of the electors in each of at least two-fifths of the counties in the State.

*Statutes*: Signatures from seven percent of the same, with the same distribution requirement, are required to place a statutory initiative on the ballot. Petitions must be filed with the Secretary of State four months before the election. The same measure may not be submitted to voters, in any form, more than once every three years.

## Passage Requirement

A majority of the votes cast in favor of the proposal equaling at least thirty-five percent of the total number of votes cast in the election is required for adoption.

**Summary of Activity from 1976 to 1992:**

| | Passed | Failed | Total |
|---|---|---|---|
| Const. amendments | 3 | 2 | 5 |
| Statutes | 0 | 3 | 3 |
| Total | 3 | 5 | 8 |

## Source

Office of the Nebraska Secretary of State, *Abstract of Votes*, 1978-1992; cite Nebraska Blue Book; Inter-University Consortium for Political and Social Research, *Referenda and Primary Election Materials, Part 20: Referenda Elections for Nebraska*, 1968-1988; Graham, *Compilation of Statewide Proposals*; Durbin, *Initiative, Referendum and Recall*; Durbin and Wolfe, *Initiative, Referendum and Recall.*

# NEVADA

## What May Be Initiated

Direct initiation of constitutional amendments and indirect initiation of statutes through the legislature has been available to voters since 1912.

## Petition Requirement

*Constitutional Amendments and Indirect Statutes:* Signatures from registered voters equal in number to at least ten percent of the total electors voting in the previous State election in not less than seventy-five percent of the counties are required to place either type of initiative on the ballot. Both are filed with the Secretary of State: Constitutional Amendments must be filed 90 days prior to the election and Indirect Statutes must be filed 30 days prior to the legislative session. Constitutional Amendment petitions may circulate from September 1 in the year preceding the general election until 90 days prior to the election. Indirect Statute petitions may circulate from January 1 prior to the year in which a regular session of the legislature is held until 30 days before the session.

## Passage Requirement

*Constitutional Amendments*: A majority of the votes cast in favor of the amendment proposal is required for adoption. If an amendment is passed it must be submitted to the voters at the next general election.[14]

*Indirect Statutes*: The legislature has 40 days to act on the initiated statute. If adopted, it can be subject to the referendum procedure; if rejected or left idle, it is submitted to the voters. If a legislative substitute is adopted, both the substitute and the original are both submitted to the voters.

**Summary of Activity from 1976 to 1992:**

| | Passed | Failed | Total |
|---|---|---|---|
| Const. amendments | 2 | 3 | 5 |
| Statutes | 0 | 2 | 2 |
| Total | 2 | 5 | 7 |

[14] This requirement (Assembly Joint Resolution No. 11 of the Fiftieth Session) was adopted by voters in 1962. No constitutional amendments initiated by petition appeared on the ballot between 1960 and 1978.

### Source

Office of the Nevada Secretary of State, History of State Initiatives, 1918-1990; Office of the Secretary of State, Nevada Ballot Questions, 1992; Statutes of the State of Nevada passed at the Fifty-First Session of the Legislature, 1961, Carson City: Jack McCarthy, State Printer, 1961, pp. 813-17; Inter-University Consortium for Political and Social Research, Referenda and Primary Election Materials, Part 42: Referenda Elections for Nevada, 1968-1988; Graham, Compilation of Statewide Proposals; Durbin, Initiative, Referendum and Recall; Durbin and Wolfe, Initiative, Referendum and Recall.

## NORTH DAKOTA

### What May Be Initiated

Direct initiation of both constitutional amendments and statutes has been available to voters since 1918. Indirect initiation of amendments and statutes was available in 1914, and utilized to make the procedures less restrictive.

### Petition Requirement

*Constitutional Amendments*: Signatures from at least four percent of the resident population are required to place a constitutional amendment on the ballot.

*Statutes*: Signatures from two percent of the same are required to place statutes on the ballot.[15] Petitions must be filed with the Secretary of State at least 90 days before a statewide election.

### Passage Requirement

A majority of the votes cast in favor of the proposal is required for adoption for both constitutional amendments and statutes.

[15] Prior to 1979, petitions for constitutional amendments were required to contain 20,000 signatures of qualified electors and petitions for constitutional amendments were required to contain 10,000 signatures of qualified electors. The change of the signature requirement to a fraction of the resident population was passed by the legislature in 1977, approved by the vote of the people November 7, 1978 and became effective January 1, 1979.

**Summary of Activity from 1976 to 1992:**

| | Passed | Failed | Total |
|---|---|---|---|
| Const. amendments | 1 | 3 | 4 |
| Statutes | 8 | 13 | 21 |
| Memorial | 1 | 0 | 1 |
| Total | 10 | 16 | 26 |

## Source

Office of the North Dakota Secretary of State, Election Returns, 1976-1992 and reference to the Constitution of North Dakota, Article III, Sections 4 and 9; Inter-University Consortium for Political and Social Research, *Referenda and Primary Election Materials, Part 21: Referenda Elections for North Dakota* 1968-1988; Graham, *Compilation of Statewide Proposals*; Durbin, *Initiative, Referendum and Recall*; Durbin and Wolfe, *Initiative, Referendum and Recall.*

# OHIO

## What May Be Initiated

Direct initiation of constitutional amendments and indirect initiation of statutes through the legislature has been available to voters since 1912.

## Petition Requirement

*Constitutional Amendments*: Signatures from registered voters equal in number to not less than ten percent of the total electors in the State, based on the previous gubernatorial election, are requited to place a constitutional amendment on the ballot.

*Indirect Statutes*: The initial petition must include three percent of the same; a supplementary petition containing an additional three percent of the electorate is required in the event the proposed statute is defeated, amended or left idle by the legislature. Both are filed with the Secretary of State: constitutional amendments must be filed 90 days prior to the election and statutes must be filed ten days prior to the legislative session.

## Passage Requirement

*Constitutional Amendments*: A majority of the votes cast in favor of the amendment proposal is required for adoption.

*Indirect Statutes*: If adopted by the general assembly, a proposal can be subject to the referendum procedure; it rejected, amended, or left idle by the legislature for four months, if can be submitted to the voters if a supplementary petition is filed, in which case a majority of the votes cast in favor of the amendment proposal is required for adoption.

**Summary of Activity from 1976 to 1992:**

| | Passed | Failed | Total |
|---|---|---|---|
| Const. amendments | 4 | 13 | 17 |
| Statutes | 0 | 2 | 2 |
| Total | 4 | 15 | 19 |

## Source

Bob Taft, Office of the Ohio Secretary of State, *Voter Participation in Constitutional Amendment and Legislation,* 1912-92; Office of the Secretary of State, Ballot Summaries, 1976-92; Inter-University Consortium for Political and Social Research, *Referenda and Primary Election Materials, Part 14: Referenda Elections for Ohio,* 1968-1988; Graham, *Compilation of Statewide Proposals*; Durbin, *Initiative, Referendum and Recall*; Durbin and Wolfe, *Initiative, Referendum and Recall.*

# OKLAHOMA

## What May Be Initiated

Direct initiation of both constitutional amendments and statutes has been available to voters since 1907, when Oklahoma joined the Union.

## Petition Requirement

*Constitutional Amendments*: Signatures from registered voters equal in number to not less than 15 percent of the total vote case in the last general election for the State officer receiving the highest number of votes are required to place a constitutional amendment on the ballot.

*Statutes*: Signatures from eight percent of the same are required to place a statutory on the ballot. Petitions are filed with the Secretary of State 90 days from the date the petition is opened for signatures.

## Passage Requirement

For both initiated constitutional amendments and statutes, a majority of the votes cast in favor of the amendment proposal is required for adoption.[16]

**Summary of Activity from 1976 to 1992:**

| | Passed | Failed | Total |
|---|---|---|---|
| Const. amendments | 5 | 1 | 6 |
| Statutes | 2 | 3 | 5 |
| Total | 7 | 4 | 11 |

## Source

Oklahoma Department of Libraries, *Oklahoma Almanac 1993-94*; Office of the Oklahoma Secretary of State, *Official Returns Special Election*, October 15, 1991 and March 10, 1992; Inter-University Consortium for Political and Social Research, *Referenda and Primary Election Materials, Part 35: Referenda Elections for Oklahoma,* 1968-1988; Graham, *Compilation of Statewide Proposals*; Durbin, *Initiative, Referendum and Recall*; Durbin and Wolfe, *Initiative, Referendum and Recall.*

# OREGON

## What May Be Initiated

Direct initiation of both constitutional amendments and statutes has been available to voters since 1902.

## Petition Requirement

*Constitutional Amendments*: Signatures of registered voters equal in number to at least eight percent of the total votes cast for Governor at the last gubernatorial election at which a governor was elected for a four-year term are required to place a constitutional amendment on the ballot.

[16] Prior to adoption of a constitutional amendment referred by the legislature in August 1974, initiated amendments and statutes which appeared in a general election had to receive a majority of the total votes cast in that general election.

*Statutes*: Signatures from six percent of the same are required to place a statutory on the ballot. Petitions must be filed with the Secretary of State at least four months before the election.

### Passage Requirement

Both initiated constitutional amendments and statutes require a majority of the votes cast in favor of the proposal in question for adoption.

**Summary of Activity from 1976 to 1992:**

| | Passed | Failed | Total |
|---|---|---|---|
| Const. amendments | 5 | 13 | 18 |
| Statutes | 15 | 24 | 39 |
| Memorial | 1 | 0 | 1 |
| Total | 21 | 37 | 58 |

### Source

Office of the Oregon Secretary of State, Summary of Election Returns, 1976-1992; Office of the Secretary of State, *Voters' Pamphlet*, 1976-1992; Inter-University Consortium for Political and Social Research, *Referenda and Primary Election Materials, Part 47: Referenda Elections for Oregon,* 1968-1988; Graham, *Compilation of Statewide Proposals*; Durbin, *Initiative, Referendum and Recall*; Durbin and Wolfe, *Initiative, Referendum and Recall.*

## South Dakota

### What May Be Initiated

Direct initiation of both constitutional amendments and indirect initiation of statutes through the legislature has been available to voters since 1898.

### Petition Requirement

*Constitutional Amendments*: Signatures from registered voters equal in number to at least ten percent of the total votes cast for Governor in the previous gubernatorial election are required to place a constitutional amendment on the ballot.

*Statutes*: Signatures from five percent of the same are required to submit a statute to the legislature. There is no requirement for a supplementary petition. Both are field with the Secretary of State: petitions for constitutional amendments must be filed at least one year prior to the election, and statutes must be filed by the first Tuesday in May in the general election year. All signatures must have been gathered within one year prior to tiling.

## Passage Requirement

*Constitutional Amendments*: A majority of the votes cast in favor of the amendment proposal is required for adoption.

*Indirect Statutes*: Whether enacted by the legislature or not, statutes are submitted to the electorate, and a majority favorable vote is sufficient for adoption

**Summary of Activity from 1976 to 1992:**

| | Passed | Failed | Total |
|---|---|---|---|
| Const. amendments | 3 | 3 | 6 |
| Statutes | 7 | 8 | 15 |
| Memorial | 0 | 1 | 1 |
| Total | 10 | 12 | 22 |

## Source

Office of the South Dakota Secretary of State, *General Election Ballot Questions,* 1980-1992; Inter-University Consortium for Political and Social Research, *Referenda and Primary Election Materials, Part 22: Referenda Elections for Nebraska,* 1968-1988; Graham, *Compilation of Statewide Proposals*; Durbin, *Initiative, Referendum and Recall*; Durbin and Wolfe, *Initiative, Referendum and Recall.*

# UTAH

## What May Be Initiated

The Utah constitution was amended in 1900 to include both direct and indirect initiation of statutes. Enabling legislation was not passed until 1917, however. Constitutional amendments may not be submitted to the ballot through the initiative process.

## Petition Requirement

*Direct Statutes*: Signatures of legal voters equal in number to ten percent of the votes cast for all candidates for Governor in the next preceding gubernatorial election are required to place a direct statute on the ballot.

*Indirect Statutes*: The initial petition must contain signatures from five percent of the same total. If the legislature rejects or does not enact the proposed statute, a supplemental petition containing additional signatures of same equal to ten percent of the votes cast for all candidates for governor in the next preceding gubernatorial election are required to qualify the indirect statue to ballot. Both are filed with the Lieutenant Governor; direct statutes must be filed at least four months prior to the election and indirect statutes must be filed at least ten days before the commencement of the annual general legislative session.

## Passage Requirement

*Direct Statutes*: A majority of the votes cast in favor of the amendment proposal is required for adoption.

*Indirect Statutes*: The legislature may pass or reject the proposed statute; it may not amend it. Enacted indirect statues may be subject to the referendum procedure. Those not enacted may be submitted to the electorate upon the filing of a supplemental petition, in which case a majority of the votes cast in favor of the amendment proposal is required for adoption.

**Summary of Activity from 1976 to 1992:**

| | Passed | Failed | Total |
|---|---|---|---|
| Direct Statutes[17] | 1 | 10 | 11 |

## Source

Office of the Utah Secretary of State, *General Election Report*, 1976-1992; *Utah Voter Information Pamphlet: General Election*, November 3, 1992, compiled by W. Val Oveson, Lieutenant Governor; Office of the Governor, *Initiative Petition History*; Inter-University Consortium for Political and Social Research, *Referenda and Primary Election Materials, Part 44: Referenda Elections for Utah,* 1968-1988; Graham, *Compilation of Statewide Proposals*; Durbin, *Initiative, Referendum and Recall*; Durbin and Wolfe, *Initiative, Referendum and Recall.*

[17] No Indirect Statues initiated by citizens appeared on the ballot in this period.

# WASHINGTON

## What May Be Initiated

Both direct and indirect initiation of statutes has been available to voters since 1912. Constitutional amendments may not be submitted to the ballot through the initiative process.

## Petition Requirement

For either direct or indirect statutes, signatures of legal voters equal in number to at least eight percent of the total votes cast for the office of Governor in the last gubernatorial election are required to place a statute on the ballot. Both are filed with the Secretary of State: direct statute proposals must be filed within ten months of the election at which they are to be voted upon, and the corresponding completed petitions must be filed at least four months prior to the election; they may circulate for a maximum of six months. Indirect statutes must be filed ten days before the next regular session of the legislature and petitions may circulate for ten months, less these ten days. The legislature may also propose a substitute to be submitted to voters by the same election as the initiative.

## Passage Requirement

*At the Polls*: For either direct or indirect statutes on the ballot, a majority of the votes cast in favor thereof is sufficient for passage if the total votes cast on the initiated statute equal at least one-third of the total votes cast in that election.

*In the Legislature*: If an indirect statute is rejected or no action is taken, the statue is submitted to the electorate at the next election and is subject to the voting rule above. If the legislature rejects the statue and adopts a substitute, both the original and the substitute appear on the ballot and are subject to the voting rule above. Indirect statutes adopted by the legislature may be subject to a referendum.

**Summary of Activity from 1976 to 1992:**

| | Passed | Failed | Total |
|---|---|---|---|
| Direct Statutes | 9 | 10 | 19 |
| Indirect Statutes | 6 | 5 | 11 |
| Memorial | 1 | 0 | 1 |
| Total | 16 | 15 | 31 |

## Source

Office of the Washington Secretary of State, *Abstract of Votes*, 1976-1992; Office of the Secretary of State, *Voter's Pamphlets*, 1976-1992; Inter-University Consortium for Political and Social Research, *Referenda and Primary Election Materials, Part 48: Referenda Elections for Washington,* 1968-1988; Graham, *Compilation of Statewide Proposals*; Durbin, *Initiative, Referendum and Recall*; Durbin and Wolfe, *Initiative, Referendum and Recall.*

# WYOMING

## What May Be Initiated

Direct initiation of statutes has been available to voters since 1968. Constitutional amendments may not be submitted to the ballot through the initiative process.

## Petition Requirement

Signatures from qualified registered electors equal in number to fifteen percent of the total votes cast in the preceding general election, from residents in at least two-thirds of the counties, are required to place a statute on the ballot. Petitions are filed with the Secretary of State at any time, but the Secretary may submit the initiative to a ballot not less than 120 days after the adjournment of the legislative session following the filing. If a similar measure has been enacted by the legislature before the election, the petition is void. The measure cannot be substantially similar to an initiative defeated within the preceding five years. A refundable $100 deposit must accompany the filing application and petitions may circulate for no more than 18 months.

## Passage Requirement

Favorable votes equal in number to more than 50 percent of the votes cast in the general election are required for adoption.

**Summary of Activity from 1976 to 1992:**[18]

| | Passed | Failed | Total |
|---|---|---|---|
| Direct Statutes | 3 | 0 | 3 |

[18] 1992 was the first year Initiatives by Petition appeared on the Wyoming ballot.

## Sources

Office of the Wyoming Secretary of State, *Official Vote,* 1992; Office of the Secretary of State, State Ballot, 1992; Inter-University Consortium for Political and Social Research, *Referenda and Primary Election Materials, Part 45: Referenda Elections for Wyoming,* 1968-1988; Graham, *Compilation of Statewide Proposals*; Durbin, *Initiative, Referendum and Recall*; Durbin and Wolfe, *Initiative, Referendum and Recall.*

## Statistical Summary: Initiatives by State, 1976-1992

The following tables identify individual petitioned initiatives appearing on the ballots of all States. The tables present the date, the topic, and the voting result of each such proposition.

## Alaska Initiatives: 1976-1992

| Date | Code | No. | Ballot proposition | Result | Yes Votes Number | Yes Votes Pct. | No Votes Number | No Votes Pct. |
|---|---|---|---|---|---|---|---|---|
| | | | **Direct statute** | | | | | |
| 11/02/76 | oth | 5 | Regulate entry into fisheries. | F | 44,304 | 37.1% | 75,125 | 62.9% |
| 11/02/76 | red | 6 | Unicameral legislature: advisory. | P | 58,782 | 51.6% | 55,204 | 48.4% |
| 11/07/78 | oth | 3 | Relocate State capital. | P | 69,414 | 55.7% | 55,253 | 44.3% |
| | oth | 4 | Disposal of State lands. | P | 70,409 | 55.9% | 55,511 | 44.1% |
| | bev | 5 | Beverage container deposits. | F | 49,882 | 39.8% | 75,397 | 60.2% |
| 11/04/80 | oth | | Alaska Stock Ownership Corp. | F | 72,072 | 47.9% | 78,404 | 52.1% |
| 11/02/82 | oth | 5 | State ownership of Federal land. | P | 136,633 | 72.9% | 50,791 | 27.1% |
| | abo | 6 | Abortion: limit State funding. | F | 77,829 | 40.8% | 113,005 | 59.2% |
| | oth | 7 | Consumption of fish and game. | F | 79,679 | 41.6% | 111,770 | 58.4% |
| 11/06/84 | oth | | Regulate transportation. | P | 116,891 | 59.8% | 78,663 | 40.2% |
| 11/08/88 | oth | 2 | Civil liability. | P | 138,511 | 71.9% | 54,206 | 28.1% |
| | edu | 3 | Separate Comm. College from Univ. | F | 83,472 | 44.4% | 104,719 | 55.6% |
| 08/28/90 | oth | | Amendments to Alaska Railroad. | F | 31,612 | 22.8% | 107,269 | 77.2% |
| 08/28/90 | lot | | Regulate gambling. | F | 50,446 | 35.7% | 90,827 | 64.3% |
| 11/06/90 | cri | | Penalties for marijuana sale/use. | P | 105,263 | 54.3% | 88,644 | 45.7% |
| | | | Total Attempted 15 | | | | | |
| | | | Total Passed 7 | | | | | |
| | | | **Memorial** | | | | | |
| 08/26/86 | nw | 1 | Nuclear Weapons Freeze. | P | 80,326 | 58.4% | 57,125 | 41.6% |
| | | | Total Attempted 1 | | | | | |
| | | | Total Passed 1 | | | | | |

## Arizona Initiatives: 1976-1992

| Date | Code | No. | Ballot Proposition | Result | Yes Votes | | No Votes | |
|---|---|---|---|---|---|---|---|---|
| | | | | | Number | Pct. | Number | Pct. |
| | | | **Constitutional amendments** | | | | | |
| 11/04/80 | bud | 106 | Property tax- 2/3 legislature. | F | 247,107 | 30.2% | 570,820 | 69.8% |
| 11/06/84 | hea | 110 | Health care institutions. | F | 372,879 | 40.5% | 547,279 | 59.5% |
| 11/04/86 | hea | 103 | Public health, safety and welfare. | F | 418,691 | 49.1% | 434,029 | 50.9% |
| 11/08/88 | eng | 106 | English as official language. | P | 584,459 | 50.5% | 572,800 | 49.5% |
| 11/06/90 | edu | 103 | Classroom Improvement program. | F | 354,733 | 34.0% | 687,977 | 66.0% |
| | cri | 104 | Victims' rights. | P | 589,870 | 57.1% | 443,930 | 42.9% |
| | con | 105 | Vehicle accident compensation law. | F | 180,922 | 17.3% | 865,289 | 82.7% |
| 11/02/92 | ter | 107 | Term limits: executive, legislators. | P | 1,026,830 | 74.2% | 356,799 | 25.8% |
| | bud | 108 | Public debt, revenue and taxation. | P | 975,191 | 71.9% | 381,777 | 28.1% |
| | abo | 110 | Preborn child protection amendment; abortion. | F | 447,654 | 31.5% | 975,251 | 68.5% |
| | | | Total Attempted 10 | | | | | |
| | | | Total Passed 4 | | | | | |
| | | | **Direct statutes** | | | | | |
| 11/02/76 | np | 200 | Legislative approval-nuclear facilities. | F | 207,639 | 29.9% | 487,795 | 70.1% |
| 11/04/80 | lot | 200 | Provisions for State lottery. | P | 412,992 | 50.9% | 398,437 | 49.1% |
| 11/02/82 | bev | 200 | Deposit/refund for beverage containers. | F | 223,825 | 31.9% | 477,856 | 68.1% |
| | oth | 201 | Declare last Sunday in May as Peace Sunday. | F | 273,146 | 40.7% | 397,462 | 59.3% |
| | vot | 202 | Voter registration by driver's license. | P | 347,559 | 51.1% | 331,985 | 48.9% |
| | oth | 203 | Repeal State control over public lands. | F | 280,285 | 42.9% | 373,290 | 57.1% |
| 11/06/84 | hea | 200 | Regulate cost of health care. | F | 375,982 | 40.4% | 553,676 | 59.6% |
| 11/04/86 | cam | 200 | Limit campaign contributions. | P | 530,346 | 65.0% | 286,030 | 35.0% |
| 11/06/90 | bud | 200 | Arizona State Parks funded by lottery. | P | 648,046 | 62.1% | 394,952 | 37.9% |
| | con | 201 | Establish Consumer Insurance Office. | F | 231,266 | 22.0% | 820,653 | 78.0% |

**Arizona Initiatives: 1976-1992 — continued**

| Date | Code | No. | Ballot Proposition | Result | Yes Votes | | No Votes | |
|---|---|---|---|---|---|---|---|---|
| | | | | | Number | Pct. | Number | Pct. |
| | | | **Direct statutes — continued** | | | | | |
| (11/06/90) | np | 202 | Hazardous waste disposal. | F | 346,926 | 33.4% | 691,580 | 66.6% |
| | con | 203 | Motor vehicle insurance; rates and damages. | F | 156,301 | 14.9% | 892,794 | 85.1% |
| 11/02/92 | oth | 200 | Unlawful methods of capturing wildlife. | F | 545,977 | 38.0% | 889,722 | 62.0% |

Total Attempted 13
Total Passed 4

## Arkansas Initiatives: 1976-1992

| Date | Code | No. | Ballot Proposition | Result | Yes Votes Number | Yes Votes Pct. | No Votes Number | No Votes Pct. |
|---|---|---|---|---|---|---|---|---|
| | | | **Constitutional amendments** | | | | | |
| 11/02/76 | oth | 59 | Rights of Labor amendment. | F | 257,111 | 35.6% | 465,343 | 64.4% |
| 11/07/78 | bud | 59 | Food and medicine sales tax exemptions. | F | 220,128 | 44.7% | 272,526 | 55.3% |
| 11/04/80 | oth | 60 | Max interest rate by 2/3 vote of legislature. | F | 327,172 | 44.0% | 416,155 | 56.0% |
| 11/02/82 | | 63 | Utility regulation amendment. Not on ballot. | | | | | |
| 11/06/84 | red | 64 | Four year terms: State constitutional officers. | P | 499,083 | 64.2% | 277,735 | 35.8% |
| | | 65 | Public funding of abortions. Not on ballot. | | | | | |
| | lot | 66 | Gambling in Garland County. | F | 236,625 | 29.6% | 561,825 | 70.4% |
| | bud | 67 | Sales/use tax for Fish and Game Commission. | F | 350,276 | 44.7% | 434,114 | 55.3% |
| 11/04/86 | abo | 65 | Abortions: limit public funding. | F | 318,007 | 50.0% | 318,523 | 50.0% |
| | red | 66 | Four year terms: elected county officials. | F | 307,425 | 48.9% | 320,981 | 51.1% |
| | bud | 67 | Issuance of revenue bonds without election. | P | 318,920 | 53.6% | 275,888 | 46.4% |
| 11/08/88 | abo | 3 | Prevent abortion funding, restrict abortion. | P | 398,107 | 52.0% | 368,117 | 48.0% |
| | bud | 4 | Repeal property tax on household goods. | F | 284,487 | 37.6% | 471,959 | 62.4% |
| 11/06/90 | | 4 | State lottery. Struck from ballot by Court. | | | | | |
| 11/03/92 | ter | 4 | Arkansas term limitations. | P | 494,326 | 59.9% | 330,836 | 40.1% |
| | | | Total Attempted | 12 | | | | |
| | | | Total Passed | 4 | | | | |
| | | | **Direct statutes** | | | | | |
| 11/04/80 | edu | 1 | Equal education for all children in State. | F | 314,105 | 44.2% | 396,821 | 55.8% |
| 11/08/88 | cam | 1 | Conduct and disclosure act: lobbyists, State officials. | P | 428,134 | 62.3% | 258,704 | 37.7% |
| 11/06/90 | cam | 1 | Conduct and disclosure act: candidates, campaigns. | P | 355,957 | 65.7% | 186.204 | 34.3% |
| | | | Total Attempted | 3 | | | | |
| | | | Total Passed | 2 | | | | |

## California Initiatives: 1976-1992

| Date | Code | No. | Ballot Proposition | Result | Yes Votes | | No Votes | |
|---|---|---|---|---|---|---|---|---|
| | | | | | Number | Pct. | Number | Pct. |
| | | | **Constitutional amendments (* = also statute)** | | | | | |
| 06/06/78 | bud | 13 | Property tax limit. | P | 4,280,689 | 64.8% | 2,326,167 | 35.2% |
| 11/06/79 | bud | 4 | Limit government appropriations. | P | 2,580,720 | 74.3% | 891,157 | 25.7% |
| 11/03/80 | bud | 9 | Taxation: indexing, business inventory exemption. | F | 2,538,667 | 39.2% | 3,942,248 | 60.8% |
| | oth | 10 | Rent control through local ordinance. | F | 2,247,395 | 35.5% | 4,090,180 | 64.5% |
| 06/08/82 | cri | 8 | Criminal justice.* | P | 2,826,081 | 56.4% | 2,182,710 | 43.6% |
| 11/02/82 | red | 14 | Districting Commission. | F | 2,840,154 | 37.2% | 4,799,586 | 62.8% |
| 11/06/84 | bud | 36 | Taxation. | F | 4,052,993 | 45.2% | 4,904,372 | 54.8% |
| | lot | 37 | State lottery.* | P | 5,398,096 | 57.9% | 3,924,346 | 42.1% |
| | red | 39 | Reapportionment.* | F | 3,995,762 | 44.8% | 4,919,860 | 55.2% |
| 11/04/86 | oth | 61 | Compensation: public employees, contractors.* | F | 2,341,883 | 34.1% | 4,523,563 | 65.9% |
| | eng | 63 | English as official State language. | P | 5,138,577 | 73.2% | 1,876,639 | 26.8% |
| 06/07/88 | bud | 71 | Appropriations limit adjustment. | F | 2,544,731 | 48.9% | 2,662,463 | 51.1% |
| | bud | 72 | Emergency reserve. Transportation. | F | 2,046,358 | 38.5% | 3,264,653 | 61.5% |
| 11/08/88 | bud | 98 | General fund financing: school funding.* | P | 4,628,737 | 50.7% | 4,500,503 | 49.3% |
| | bud | 99 | Cigarette and tobacco tax. Benefit fund. | P | 5,607,387 | 58.2% | 4,032,644 | 41.8% |
| 06/05/90 | cri | 115 | Criminal law.* | P | 2,690,115 | 57.0% | 2,026,600 | 43.0% |
| | red | 118 | Legislature. Reapportionment. Ethics.* | F | 1,615,164 | 33.0% | 3,281,178 | 67.0% |
| | red | 119 | Reapportionment by commission. | F | 1,761,510 | 36.2% | 3,105,502 | 63.8% |
| 11/06/90 | cri | 129 | Drug enforcement, prevention, treatment, prisons.* | F | 1,982,369 | 27.6% | 5,192,742 | 72.4% |
| | ter | 131 | Term limits. Ethics. Campaign financing.* | F | 2,723,763 | 37.8% | 4,490,973 | 62.2% |
| | oth | 132 | Marine resources. | P | 3,959,238 | 55.8% | 3,140,773 | 44.2% |
| | bud | 134 | Alcohol surtax. | F | 2,284,256 | 31.0% | 5,076,822 | 69.0% |
| | bud | 136 | State, local taxation. | F | 3,439,621 | 47.9% | 3,744,620 | 52.1% |
| | vot | 137 | Initiative and referendum process. | F | 3,157,383 | 45.0% | 3,860,756 | 55.0% |
| | cri | 139 | Prison inmate labor. Tax credit. | P | 3,867,147 | 54.0% | 3,288,144 | 46.0% |
| | ter | 140 | Term limits, retirement, operating costs. | P | 3,744,447 | 52.2% | 3,432,666 | 47.8% |

**California Initiatives: 1976-1992 — continued**

| Date | Code | No. | Ballot Proposition | Result | Yes Votes Number | Yes Votes Pct. | No Votes Number | No Votes Pct. |
|---|---|---|---|---|---|---|---|---|
| | | | **Constitutional Initiatives — continued** | | | | | |
| 11/03/92 | bud | 162 | Public employee retirement systems. | P | 5,066,529 | 51.0% | 4,867,680 | 49.0% |
| | bud | 163 | End taxation of certain food products.* | P | 6,967,007 | 66.6% | 3,491,372 | 33.4% |
| | bud | 165 | Budget; welfare. Procedural & substantive changes.* | F | 4,869,305 | 46.6% | 5,577,059 | 53.4% |
| | | | Total Attempted 29 | | | | | |
| | | | Total Passed 13 | | | | | |
| | | | **Direct Statutes** | | | | | |
| 06/08/76 | np | 15 | Nuclear power plants. | F | 1,950,430 | 32.5% | 4,048,355 | 67.5% |
| 11/02/76 | lot | 13 | Greyhound dog racing. | F | 1,883,032 | 24.6% | 5,766,315 | 75.4% |
| | oth | 14 | Agricultural labor relations. | F | 2,915,981 | 37.8% | 4,791,966 | 62.2% |
| 11/07/78 | oth | 5 | Regulation of smoking. | F | 3,125,148 | 45.6% | 3,721,682 | 54.4% |
| | sex | 6 | School employees; homosexuality. | F | 2,823,148 | 41.6% | 3,969,120 | 58.4% |
| | cri | 7 | Murder. Penalty. | P | 4,480,275 | 71.1% | 1,818,357 | 28.9% |
| 06/03/80 | bud | 11 | Taxation. 10% surtax on energy businesses. | F | 2,821,150 | 44.3% | 3,544,840 | 55.7% |
| 11/04/80 | oth | 10 | Smoking and non-smoking sections. | F | 3,861,614 | 46.6% | 4,432,209 | 53.4% |
| 06/08/82 | bud | 5 | Gift and inheritance taxes. (Miller) | P | 3,208,394 | 61.8% | 1,983,818 | 38.2% |
| | bud | 6 | Gift and inheritance taxes. (Rogers) | P | 3,330,547 | 64.4% | 1,838,128 | 35.6% |
| | bud | 7 | Income tax indexing. | P | 3,191,178 | 63.5% | 1,835,054 | 36.5% |
| 11/02/82 | bev | 11 | Beverage containers. | F | 3,359,281 | 44.1% | 4,256,174 | 55.9% |
| | uti | 13 | Water resources. | F | 2,497,200 | 35.2% | 4,599,103 | 64.8% |
| | cri | 15 | Handgun registration. | F | 2,840,154 | 37.2% | 4,799,586 | 62.8% |
| 06/05/84 | red | 24 | Legislature: rules, procedures, powers, funding. | P | 2,444,751 | 53.1% | 2,162,024 | 46.9% |
| 11/06/84 | | 35 | Balance Federal budget. Removed from ballot by Court. | | | | | |
| | eng | 38 | Voting materials, English only. | P | 6,390,676 | 70.7% | 2,645,599 | 29.3% |
| | cam | 40 | Campaign contribution limits. State offices. | F | 3,109,746 | 35.5% | 5,640,473 | 64.5% |

**California Initiatives: 1976-1992 — continued**

| Date | Code | No. | Ballot Proposition | Result | Yes Votes Number | Yes Votes Pct. | No Votes Number | No Votes Pct. |
|---|---|---|---|---|---|---|---|---|
| | | | **Direct Statutes — continued** | | | | | |
| (11/06/84) | hea | 41 | Public aid, medical assistance programs. | F | 3,247,127 | 37.0% | 5,517,210 | 63.0% |
| 06/03/86 | oth | 51 | Multiple defendants tort damage liability. | P | 2,875,382 | 62.1% | 1,753,244 | 37.9% |
| 11/04/86 | bud | 62 | Taxation, local governments and districts. | P | 3,858,119 | 58.0% | 2,798,805 | 42.0% |
| | sex | 64 | Acquired Immune Deficiency Syndrome (AIDS). | F | 2,039,744 | 28.9% | 5,012,255 | 71.1% |
| | np | 65 | Toxic discharge into drinking water. | P | 4,400,471 | 62.6% | 2,632,617 | 37.4% |
| 06/07/88 | cam | 68 | Legislative campaigns-spending/contribution limits. | P | 2,802,614 | 52.8% | 2,501,263 | 47.2% |
| | sex | 69 | Acquired Immune Deficiency Syndrome (AIDS). | F | 1,746,780 | 32.0% | 3,718,776 | 68.0% |
| | cam | 73 | Campaign bunding. | P | 3,144,944 | 58.1% | 2,271,941 | 41.9% |
| 11/08/88 | oth | 95 | Hunger and homelessness. Funding. | F | 4,090,441 | 45.2% | 4,962,409 | 54.8% |
| | oth | 96 | Communicable disease tests. | P | 5,758,670 | 62.4% | 3,468,215 | 37.6% |
| | hea | 97 | State occupational safety and health plan. | P | 4,776,182 | 53.7% | 4,116,102 | 46.3% |
| | con | 100 | Insurance rates, regulation. | F | 3,849,572 | 40.9% | 5,562,483 | 59.1% |
| | con | 101 | Automobile accident claims, insurance rates. | F | 1,226,735 | 13.3% | 8,020,659 | 86.7% |
| | sex | 102 | Reporting exposure to AIDS virus. | F | 3,208,517 | 34.4% | 6,116,276 | 65.6% |
| | con | 103 | Insurance rates, regulation, Commission. | P | 4,844,312 | 51.1% | 4,630,752 | 48.9% |
| | con | 104 | Automobile and other insurance. | F | 2,391,287 | 25.4% | 7,015,325 | 74.6% |
| | oth | 105 | Disclosure to consumers, voters, investors. | P | 4,846,674 | 54.5% | 4,046,654 | 45.5% |
| | oth | 106 | Attorney fee limit for tort claims. | F | 4,288,346 | 46.9% | 4,855,839 | 53.1% |
| 06/05/90 | oth | 116 | Rail transportation. | P | 2,579,810 | 53.3% | 2,263,574 | 46.7% |
| | oth | 117 | Wildlife protection. | P | 2,572,470 | 52.4% | 2,334,900 | 47.6% |
| 11/06/90 | hea | 128 | Environment. Public health. | F | 2,636,663 | 35.6% | 4,760,022 | 64.4% |
| | bud | 130 | Forest acquisition. Timber harvesting. Bond Act. | F | 3,528,887 | 47.9% | 3,842,733 | 52.1% |
| | cri | 133 | Drug enforcement and prevention. | F | 2,281,937 | 31.9% | 4,877,808 | 68.1% |
| | oth | 135 | Pesticide regulation. | F | 2,191,301 | 30.4% | 5,015,928 | 69.6% |
| | bud | 138 | Forest acquisition. Timber harvesting. Bond Act. | F | 2,108,389 | 28.8% | 5,201,891 | 71.2% |

## California Initiatives: 1976-1992 — continued

| Date | Code | No. | Ballot Proposition | | Result | Yes Votes | | No Votes | |
|---|---|---|---|---|---|---|---|---|---|
| | | | | | | Number | Pct. | Number | Pct. |
| | | | **Direct statutes — continued** | | | | | | |
| 11/03/92 | oth | 161 | Physician-assisted death. Terminal condition. | | F | 4,863,478 | 45.9% | 5,739,916 | 54.1% |
| | ter | 164 | Congressional term limits. | | P | 6,578,636 | 63.6% | 3,769,510 | 36.4% |
| | hea | 166 | Basic health care coverage. | | F | 3,255,301 | 30.8% | 7,310,636 | 69.2% |
| | bud | 167 | State taxes. | | F | 4,293,460 | 41.2% | 6,136,893 | 58.8% |
| | | | Total Attempted | 46 | | | | | |
| | | | Total Passed | 18 | | | | | |
| | | | **Memorial** | | | | | | |
| 11/02/82 | nw | 12 | Nuclear weapons. | | P | 3,871,345 | 52.3% | 3,528,463 | 47.7% |
| | | | Total Attempted | 1 | | | | | |
| | | | Total Passed | 1 | | | | | |
| | | | **Bonds** | | | | | | |
| 06/07/88 | bud | 70 | Conservation Bond Act. | | P | 3,531,629 | 65.1% | 1,889,346 | 34.9% |
| | | | Total Attempted | 1 | | | | | |
| | | | Total Passed | 1 | | | | | |

## Colorado Initiatives: 1976-1992

| Date | Code | No. | Ballot Proposition | Result | Yes Votes | | No Votes | |
|---|---|---|---|---|---|---|---|---|
| | | | | | Number | Pct. | Number | Pct. |
| | | | **Constitutional Amendments** | | | | | |
| 11/04/76 | lot | 1 | Authorize conduct of sweepstakes. | P | 522,068 | 50.5% | 511,135 | 49.5% |
| | bud | 2 | Classification/taxation of motor vehicles. | P | 627,562 | 61.8% | 388,666 | 38.2% |
| | np | 3 | Nuclear plants-legislative approval. | F | 305,142 | 29.3% | 734,843 | 70.7% |
| | oth | 4 | Exemptions from State personnel systems. | F | 237,853 | 23.6% | 768,687 | 76.4% |
| | oth | 5 | Compensation of county officials. | F | 376,386 | 37.4% | 629,136 | 62.6% |
| | bud | 10 | Voter approval: acts of new/increased taxes. | F | 259,201 | 25.3% | 767,157 | 74.7% |
| 11/07/78 | oth | 1 | Office of County Commissioner, vacancies. | P | 442,071 | 66.1% | 226,432 | 33.9% |
| | bud | 2 | State expenditure limitations. | F | 295,616 | 41.3% | 420,759 | 58.7% |
| 11/02/82 | bud | 1 | Property tax assessment. | P | 551,334 | 65.5% | 290,590 | 34.5% |
| | cri | 2 | Denial of bail. | P | 737,813 | 82.5% | 156,336 | 17.5% |
| | red | 3 | Judicial discipline. | P | 659,905 | 77.3% | 193,425 | 22.7% |
| | red | 4 | Legislative sessions. | P | 442,601 | 54.3% | 372,897 | 45.7% |
| 11/06/84 | con | 1 | Appointment of Commissioner of Insurance. | P | 641,587 | 58.8% | 449,362 | 41.2% |
| | vot | 2 | Eligibility to vote. | P | 811,130 | 72.7% | 304,208 | 27.3% |
| | abo | 3 | Abortion funding. | P | 627,343 | 50.4% | 617,637 | 49.6% |
| | lot | 5 | Casino gambling in Pueblo. | F | 406,989 | 33.2% | 819,533 | 66.8% |
| 11/04/86 | oth | 1 | Appointments by merit. | F | 461,004 | 48.6% | 488,226 | 51.4% |
| | oth | 2 | Compensation of county officers. | F | 406,960 | 45.2% | 492,511 | 54.8% |
| | vot | 3 | Franchises subject to initiative & referendum. | P | 455,053 | 53.4% | 396,738 | 46.6% |
| | bud | 4 | Voter approval for tax increases. | F | 375,097 | 37.5% | 625,158 | 62.5% |
| 11/08/88 | eng | 1 | English as official language. | P | 829,617 | 61.2% | 527,053 | 38.8% |
| | red | 2 | Reimbursement of Recall expenses. | P | 645,002 | 53.9% | 551,118 | 46.1% |
| | red | 3 | Legislative session length. | P | 641,363 | 52.3% | 584,359 | 47.7% |
| | oth | 4 | Concerning maximum eight-hour workday. | P | 799,250 | 67.2% | 389,906 | 32.8% |
| | bud | 5 | Property tax exempt: non-producing mining claims. | P | 624,021 | 51.9% | 578,295 | 48.1% |
| | bud | 6 | Voter approval: increases in tax revenues. | F | 567,884 | 42.2% | 778,075 | 57.8% |
| | abo | 7 | Funding for abortion. | F | 534,070 | 39.8% | 809,078 | 60.2% |
| | bud | 8 | Referral of measures to committees. | P | 852,448 | 72.0% | 332,159 | 28.0% |

## Colorado Initiatives: 1976-1992 — continued

| | | | | | Yes Votes | | No Votes | |
|---|---|---|---|---|---|---|---|---|
| Date | Code | No. | Ballot Proposition | Result | Number | Pct. | Number | Pct. |
| | | | **Constitutional Amendments — continued** | | | | | |
| 11/06/90 | bud | 1 | Limit taxation. | F | 494,934 | 48.9% | 516,534 | 51.1% |
| | vot | 2 | Presidential primaries: electoral votes. | P | 582,835 | 61.2% | 370,166 | 38.8% |
| | vot | 3 | Repeal obsolete constitutional provisions. | P | 717,544 | 77.8% | 204,294 | 22.2% |
| | lot | 4 | Legalizing limited gaming. | P | 574,620 | 57.3% | 428,096 | 42.7% |
| | ter | 5 | Term limits. | P | 708,975 | 71.0% | 289,664 | 29.0% |
| 11/03/92 | bud | 1 | Voter approval: tax revenue increases. | P | 812,308 | 53.7% | 700,906 | 46.3% |
| | sex | 2 | Discrimination for sexual orientation. | P | 813,966 | 53.4% | 710,151 | 46.6% |
| | lot | 3 | Limited gaming. | F | 448,779 | 29.7% | 1,060,168 | 70.3% |
| | lot | 4 | Limited gaming. | F | 414,699 | 27.6% | 1,087,136 | 72.4% |
| | lot | 5 | Limited gaming. | F | 414,489 | 27.6% | 1,087,713 | 72.4% |
| | edu | 7 | Vouchers for school funding. | F | 503,162 | 33.2% | 1,011,901 | 66.8% |
| | oth | 8 | The Great Outdoors Colorado program. | P | 876,424 | 58.2% | 629,490 | 41.8% |
| | bud | 9 | Limited gaming; surtax. | F | 292,961 | 19.6% | 1,200,336 | 80.4% |

| | |
|---|---|
| Total Attempted | 41 |
| Total Passed | 24 |

**Colorado Initiatives: 1976-1992 — continued**

| Date | Code | No. | Ballot Proposition | Result | Yes Votes Number | Yes Votes Pct. | No Votes Number | No Votes Pct. |
|---|---|---|---|---|---|---|---|---|
| | | | **Direct Statutes** | | | | | |
| 11/04/76 | sex | 6 | Repeal act providing equal rights on account of sex. | F | 401,943 | 39.0% | 629,060 | 61.0% |
| | bud | 7 | Exempt food products from sales and use taxes. | F | 406,311 | 38.9% | 639,058 | 61.1% |
| | bev | 8 | Minimum deposit on beverage containers. | F | 346,335 | 33.0% | 702,292 | 67.0% |
| | oth | 9 | Department of Public Counselor. | F | 304,594 | 30.0% | 711,627 | 70.0% |
| 11/02/82 | bev | 5 | Beverage containers. | F | 242,653 | 25.5% | 708,564 | 74.5% |
| | oth | 7 | Wine in grocery stores. | F | 333,467 | 35.0% | 620,190 | 65.0% |
| 11/06/84 | vot | 4 | Motor Voter act. | P | 705,725 | 61.2% | 447,803 | 38.8% |
| 11/03/92 | edu | 6 | Act for system of educational standards. | F | 693,231 | 45.6% | 826,787 | 54.4% |
| | oth | 10 | Prohibit taking of black bears. | P | 1,054,032 | 69.7% | 458,260 | 30.3% |
| | | | Total Attempted 9 | | | | | |
| | | | Total Passed 2 | | | | | |
| | | | **Memorial** | | | | | |
| 11/02/82 | nw | 6 | Nuclear weapons. | F | 325,985 | 36.6% | 564,606 | 63.4% |
| | | | Total Attempted 1 | | | | | |
| | | | Total Passed 0 | | | | | |

## Florida Initiatives: 1976-1992

| Date | Code | No. | Ballot Proposition | Result | Yes Votes Number | Yes Votes Pct. | No Votes Number | No Votes Pct. |
|---|---|---|---|---|---|---|---|---|
| | | | **Constitutional Amendments** | | | | | |
| 11/02/76 | cam | 1 | Sunshine amendment. | P | 1,765,626 | 79.3% | 461,940 | 20.7% |
| 11/07/78 | lot | 9 | Casino gambling. | F | 687,460 | 28.6% | 1,720,275 | 71.4% |
| 11/04/86 | lot | 2 | Casino gambling. | F | 1,036,250 | 31.7% | 2,237,555 | 68.3% |
| | lot | 5 | State operated lottery. | P | 2,039,437 | 63.6% | 1,168,858 | 36.4% |
| 11/08/88 | oth | 10 | Limit damages in civil actions. | F | 1,837,041 | 43.4% | 2,394,932 | 56.6% |
| | eng | 11 | English as official State language. | P | 3,457,039 | 83.9% | 664,861 | 16.1% |
| 11/03/92 | ter | 9 | Term Limits. | P | 3,625,500 | 76.8% | 1,097,127 | 23.2% |
| | bud | 10 | Limit homestead valuations. | P | 2,493,742 | 53.6% | 2,154,747 | 46.4% |
| | | | Total Attempted | 8 | | | | |
| | | | Total Passed | 5 | | | | |

## Idaho Initiatives: 1976-1992

| | | | | | Yes Votes | | No Votes | |
|---|---|---|---|---|---|---|---|---|
| Date | Code | No. | Ballot Proposition | Result | Number | Pct. | Number | Pct. |
| | | | **Direct Statutes** | | | | | |
| 11/07/78 | bud | 1 | Restrict property valuation or tax changes. | P | 164,817 | 58.3% | 118,102 | 41.7% |
| 11/02/82 | bud | 1 | Home improvement exemptions: ad valorem tax. | P | 168,895 | 56.5% | 130,062 | 43.5% |
| | oth | 2 | Practice of Denturitry; licensing board. | P | 197,756 | 65.2% | 105,436 | 34.8% |
| | np | 3 | Use of nuclear power for electricity generation. | P | 175,407 | 54.8% | 144,408 | 45.2% |
| 11/06/84 | bud | 1 | Sales tax exemption: food for consumption. | F | 186,505 | 47.0% | 210,054 | 53.0% |
| 11/04/86 | lot | 1 | State lottery; lottery commission. | P | 226,816 | 60.0% | 151,132 | 40.0% |
| 11/03/92 | bud | 1 | Limit ad valorem property tax rates. | F | 163,690 | 34.5% | 311,159 | 65.5% |
| | | | Total Attempted | 7 | | | | |
| | | | Total Passed | 5 | | | | |

## Illinois Initiative: 1976-1992

| Date | Code | No. | Ballot Proposition | Result | Yes Votes | | No Votes | |
|---|---|---|---|---|---|---|---|---|
| | | | | | Number | Pct. | Number | Pct. |
| | | | **Constitutional Amendment** | | | | | |
| 11/04/80 | red | | Reduce size of legislature. | P | 2,112,224 | 68.7% | 962,325 | 31.3% |
| | | | Total Attempted | 1 | | | | |
| | | | Total Passed | 1 | | | | |

## Maine Initiatives: 1976-1991

| Date | Code | No. | Ballot Proposition | Result | Yes Votes Number | Yes Votes Pct. | No Votes Number | No Votes Pct. |
|---|---|---|---|---|---|---|---|---|
| | | | **Indirect Statutes** | | | | | |
| 06/08/76 | oth | | Public preserve in Bigelow Mountain area. | P | 85,782 | 51.2% | 81,915 | 48.8% |
| 09/23/80 | np | | Prohibit electric power by nuclear fission. | F | 161,181 | 40.9% | 233,198 | 59.1% |
| 11/03/81 | oth | | Create Maine Energy Commission. | F | 90,333 | 38.4% | 144,647 | 61.6% |
| 11/02/82 | bud | | Abolish inflation-induced State income tax increases. | P | 240,023 | 56.7% | 182,939 | 43.3% |
| 11/02/82 | oth | | Repeal of milk price controls. | F | 222,422 | 48.9% | 232,430 | 51.1% |
| 11/02/82 | np | | End nuclear power for electricity in five years. | F | 201,617 | 44.0% | 256,124 | 56.0% |
| 11/08/83 | oth | | Repeal hunting season on moose. | F | 121,125 | 39.5% | 185,603 | 60.5% |
| 11/05/85 | | | Bills for low-level radioactive waste sites: | | | | | |
| | np | | -Initiated: people may vote on any disposal plan. | P | 86,678 | 50.3% | | |
| | | | -Legislative: may vote if waste not disposed of safely. | | | | 45,920 | 26.6% |
| | | | -Against both measures. | | | | 39,893 | 23.1% |
| 06/10/86 | cri | | Obscenity law. | F | 81,970 | 28.1% | 209,537 | 71.9% |
| 11/04/86 | uti | 1 | Ban mandatory local phone service; flat rates. | P | 241,894 | 57.5% | 178,745 | 42.5% |
| 11/03/87 | np | 1 | No high-waste nuclear plants after July 4, 1988. | P | 235,069 | 59.1% | 162,902 | 40.9% |
| 11/07/89 | cam | 1 | Campaign finance: candidates for Governor. | F | 98,558 | 43.9% | 126,140 | 56.1% |
| 11/06/90 | oth | 1 | Stores open on Sundays/holidays; option to workers. | P | 272,129 | 52.5% | 246,378 | 47.5% |
| 11/05/91 | oth | | Deauthorize widening of the Maine Turnpike. | P | 224,277 | 58.8% | 156,861 | 41.2% |
| | | | Total Attempted 14 | | | | | |
| | | | Total Passed 7 | | | | | |
| | | | **Memorial** | | | | | |
| 11/07/89 | nw | 2 | Stop cruise missile tests. | P | 122,820 | 52.3% | 112,109 | 47.7% |
| | | | Total Attempted 1 | | | | | |
| | | | Total Passed 1 | | | | | |

## Massachusetts Initiatives: 1976-1992

| Date | Code | No. | Ballot Proposition | Result | Yes Votes | | No Votes | |
|---|---|---|---|---|---|---|---|---|
| | | | | | Number | Pct. | Number | Pct. |
| | | | **Indirect Statutes** | | | | | |
| 11/02/76 | oth | 4 | Massachusetts Power Authority. | F | 346,727 | 14.9% | 1,983,318 | 85.1% |
| | cri | 5 | Ban on handguns. | F | 743,014 | 30.8% | 1,669,945 | 69.2% |
| | bev | 6 | Control bottles and cans. | F | 1,207,162 | 49.6% | 1,228,185 | 50.4% |
| | uti | 7 | Uniform electric rates. | F | 608,691 | 25.3% | 1,793,022 | 74.7% |
| 11/04/80 | bud | 2 | Limit local taxes. | P | 1,438,768 | 59.0% | 998,839 | 41.0% |
| | bud | 3 | Limit taxes; increase State share of education costs. | F | 816,805 | 35.7% | 1,473,804 | 64.3% |
| 11/02/82 | np | 3 | Restrict radioactive waste disposal; construction. | P | 1,249,462 | 67.5% | 602,955 | 32.5% |
| 11/04/86 | bud | 3 | Limit State revenue tax increases: income surtax. | P | 863,130 | 54.4% | 724,925 | 45.6% |
| | np | 4 | DEQE to identify/clean hazardous waste sites. | P | 1,174,676 | 74.4% | 404,521 | 25.6% |
| | vot | 6 | Mail-in voter registration. | F | 603,370 | 38.4% | 966,227 | 61.6% |
| 11/08/88 | oth | 2 | Repeal prevailing wage law. | F | 1,063,324 | 41.8% | 1,479,319 | 58.2% |
| | oth | 3 | Regulate treatment of farm animals. | F | 713,999 | 28.6% | 1,781,172 | 71.4% |
| | np | 4 | No electric power plants that produce nuclear waste. | F | 770,800 | 32.2% | 1,626,402 | 67.8% |
| 11/06/90 | oth | 2 | Limit State use of consultants. | F | 1,038,174 | 45.4% | 1,246,739 | 54.6% |
| | bud | 3 | Change income tax law, regulate State agency fees. | F | 935,337 | 40.1% | 1,397,542 | 59.9% |
| | vot | 4 | Establishment of political parties, nominations. | P | 1,134,535 | 52.5% | 1,027,966 | 47.5% |
| | bud | 5 | Regulate local aid fund. | P | 1,242,270 | 56.7% | 949,561 | 43.3% |
| 11/03/92 | bud | 1 | Tax on cigarettes and smokeless tobacco. | P | 1,429,642 | 54.4% | 1,200,438 | 45.6% |
| | bud | 2 | Public reporting of corporate tax information. | P | 1,372,192 | 55.5% | 1,099,585 | 44.5% |
| | bev | 3 | Reduced, reusable, or recyclable packaging. | F | 1,071,219 | 40.8% | 1,556,298 | 59.2% |
| | bud | 4 | Tax on oils, hazardous materials. | F | 1,051,046 | 41.4% | 1,485,451 | 58.6% |

| | |
|---|---|
| Total Attempted | 21 |
| Total Passed | 8 |

## Michigan Initiatives: 1976-1992

| Date | Code | No. | Ballot Proposition | Result | Yes Votes Number | Yes Votes Pct. | No Votes Number | No Votes Pct. |
|---|---|---|---|---|---|---|---|---|
| | | | **Constitutional Amendments** | | | | | |
| 11/02/76 | bud | C | Limit State spending. | F | 1,407,438 | 43.0% | 1,866,620 | 57.0% |
| | bud | D | Remove ban on graduated income tax. | F | 897,780 | 27.8% | 2,332,513 | 72.2% |
| 11/07/78 | cri | D | Alcohol: must be 21 to purchase/possess. | P | 1,609,589 | 57.1% | 1,208,497 | 42.9% |
| | bud | E | Tax limitation (Headlee Amendment). | P | 1,450,150 | 52.5% | 1,313,984 | 47.5% |
| | oth | G | Collective bargaining for Michigan State Troopers. | P | 1,535,023 | 56.0% | 1,203,930 | 44.0% |
| | bud | H | Exempt property tax from school operations. | F | 718,440 | 25.7% | 2,075,583 | 74.3% |
| | bud | J | Property and taxes, local mandates, voter approval. | F | 1,032,343 | 37.3% | 1,737,133 | 62.7% |
| 11/04/80 | bud | | Taxes for school finance; equal per-pupil funding. | F | 746,027 | 21.2% | 2,769,497 | 78.8% |
| | bud | | Reduce property taxes; voter approval for new taxes. | F | 1,622,301 | 44.2% | 2,051,008 | 55.8% |
| 11/02/82 | oth | | Create department of State Police in Constitution. | F | 720,915 | 25.4% | 2,111,802 | 74.6% |
| | oth | | Establish elected Public Service Commission. | F | 1,026,160 | 36.7% | 1,771,098 | 63.3% |
| 11/06/84 | bud | C | State/local tax rates set to those of 12/31/81. | F | 1,376,141 | 40.3% | 2,035,867 | 59.7% |
| 11/03/92 | ter | B | Term limits: Congressional and State offices. | P | 2,323,171 | 58.8% | 1,629,368 | 41.2% |
| | bud | C | Exempt property tax from school funds; increases. | F | 1,591,664 | 41.0% | 2,292,862 | 59.0% |

| | |
|---|---|
| Total Attempted | 14 |
| Total Passed | 4 |

**Michigan Initiatives: 1976-1992 — continued**

| Date | Code | No. | Ballot Proposition | Result | Yes Votes | | No Votes | |
|---|---|---|---|---|---|---|---|---|
| | | | | | Number | Pct. | Number | Pct. |
| | | | **Indirect Statutes** | | | | | |
| 11/02/76 | bev | A | Ban nonreturnable beverage containers; deposits. | P | 2,160,398 | 63.8% | 1,227,254 | 36.2% |
| 11/07/78 | cri | B | Limit parole-violent criminals; minimum sentence. | P | 2,075,599 | 74.5% | 711,262 | 25.5% |
| 11/02/82 | oth | | Foreclosures: no "due on sale" clauses; security. | F | 1,344,463 | 48.2% | 1,445,897 | 51.8% |
| | uti | | Hearings on utility rate increases, procedures. | P | 1,472,442 | 50.7% | 1,431,884 | 49.3% |
| 11/03/92 | con | D | Amendment of auto insurance laws. | F | 1,482,577 | 37.4% | 2,480,032 | 62.6% |
| | | | Total Attempted | 5 | | | | |
| | | | Total Passed | 3 | | | | |
| | | | **Memorial** | | | | | |
| 11/02/82 | nw | | Mutual nuclear weapons freeze with Soviet Union. | P | 1,585,809 | 56.6% | 1,216,172 | 43.4% |
| | | | Total Attempted | 1 | | | | |
| | | | Total Passed | 1 | | | | |

## Missouri Initiatives: 1976-1992

| Date | Code | No. | Ballot Proposition | Result | Yes Votes Number | Yes Votes Pct. | No Votes Number | No Votes Pct. |
|---|---|---|---|---|---|---|---|---|
| | | | **Constitutional Amendments** | | | | | |
| 08/03/76 | edu | 10 | Student assistance: public, non-public schools. | F | 463,198 | 40.3% | 684,818 | 59.7% |
| 11/02/76 | bud | 1 | Sales tax for conservation. | P | 901,535 | 50.8% | 873,421 | 49.2% |
| | bud | 2 | Exempt food and drugs from Sales tax. | F | 742,627 | 43.3% | 970,560 | 56.7% |
| 08/08/78 | bud | 5 | Increase gas tax from 7 to 10 cents. | F | 112,425 | 12.3% | 803,936 | 87.7% |
| 11/07/78 | oth | 13 | Right to work. | F | 631,829 | 40.0% | 948,387 | 60.0% |
| 11/04/80 | bud | | Limit State and local taxes. | P | 1,002,935 | 55.4% | 807,187 | 44.6% |
| 11/06/84 | lot | 7 | Horse Racing Commission; wagering; education. | P | 1,157,664 | 60.0% | 771,437 | 40.0% |
| 11/08/88 | bud | 7 | Extend of use and sales taxes. | P | 1,263,644 | 68.7% | 576,790 | 31.3% |
| | hea | 8 | Trust fund for catastrophic, high-risk illness. | F | 550,974 | 28.7% | 1,372,102 | 71.3% |
| 11/03/92 | ter | 12 | Term limits: 16 years for State legislators. | P | 1,610,311 | 75.0% | 535,562 | 25.0% |
| | ter | 13 | U.S. Senators, 2 terms; Representatives, 4 terms. | P | 1,590,552 | 74.0% | 558,299 | 26.0% |
| | | | Total Attempted 11 | | | | | |
| | | | Total Passed 6 | | | | | |
| | | | **Direct Statutes** | | | | | |
| 11/02/76 | uti | 3 | Electric utility rate base. | P | 1,132,664 | 63.1% | 663,486 | 36.9% |
| 11/04/80 | np | | Nuclear waste. | F | 772,597 | 39.1% | 1,201,821 | 60.9% |
| 11/02/82 | bud | | One cent sales tax increase. | P | 757,756 | 53.2% | 667,190 | 46.8% |
| 11/02/82 | uti | | Utility Consumers Board. | F | 513,247 | 38.6% | 815,973 | 61.4% |
| 11/06/84 | uti | B | Electricity generation cost charges for consumers. | P | 1,317,444 | 66.9% | 650,895 | 33.1% |
| 11/06/90 | oth | | Streams. | F | 320,958 | 24.9% | 969,082 | 75.1% |
| | | | Total Attempted 6 | | | | | |
| | | | Total Passed 3 | | | | | |

## Montana Initiatives: 1976-1992

| Date | Code | No. | Ballot Proposition | Result | Yes Votes Number | Yes Votes Pct. | No Votes Number | No Votes Pct. |
|---|---|---|---|---|---|---|---|---|
| | | | **Constitutional Amendments** | | | | | |
| 11/02/76 | bud | 7 | Budget ceiling. | F | 86,191 | 30.7% | 194,734 | 69.3% |
| 11/07/78 | bud | 8 | Property tax assessment and Commission. | F | 117,760 | 46.7% | 134,462 | 53.3% |
| 11/04/86 | bud | 27 | Abolish property tax; popular vote for tax change. | F | 140,090 | 44.2% | 177,016 | 55.8% |
| | oth | 30 | Concerning private liability. | P | 172,502 | 55.8% | 136,653 | 44.2% |
| 11/06/90 | bud | 55 | Repeal existing taxes; charges on business exchange. | F | 78,254 | 25.2% | 232,807 | 74.8% |
| 11/03/92 | oth | 63 | (Title not provided with canvass) | F | 165,126 | 42.9% | 219,403 | 57.1% |
| | oth | 64 | (Title not provided with canvass) | P | 264,174 | 66.9% | 130,695 | 33.1% |
| | | | Total | Attempted | 7 | | | |
| | | | Total | Passed | 2 | | | |

Total Attempted 11
Total Passed 6

| Date | Code | No. | Ballot Proposition | Result | Yes Votes Number | Yes Votes Pct. | No Votes Number | No Votes Pct. |
|---|---|---|---|---|---|---|---|---|
| | | | **Direct Statutes** | | | | | |
| 11/02/76 | np | 71 | Nuclear Facility Act. | F | 120,557 | 40.7% | 175,925 | 59.3% |
| | bud | 72 | State funded Homestead Tax Relief Act. | P | 204,532 | 71.0% | 83,611 | 29.0% |
| | red | 73 | Recall and Advisory Recall Act. | P | 155,899 | 57.4% | 115,702 | 42.6% |
| 11/07/78 | cri | 79 | Local option: obscenity laws. | P | 139,763 | 52.7% | 125,475 | 47.3% |
| | np | 80 | Voter regulation of nuclear facilities. | P | 177,778 | 65.1% | 95,179 | 34.9% |
| | oth | 81 | Table wine retail sales. | P | 169,069 | 60.1% | 112,195 | 39.9% |
| 11/04/80 | np | 84 | Prohibit disposal of radioactive waste in MT. | P | 172,909 | 50.1% | 172,493 | 49.9% |
| | cam | 85 | Lobbyist disclosure. | P | 259,698 | 77.3% | 76,358 | 22.7% |
| | bud | 86 | Tax indexing. | P | 233,497 | 69.5% | 102,635 | 30.5% |
| | bev | 87 | Montana Litter Control and Recycling Act. | F | 100,761 | 28.8% | 248,928 | 71.2% |
| 11/02/82 | lot | 92 | Expanding gambling. | F | 115,297 | 37.6% | 191,334 | 62.4% |
| | oth | 94 | Beer and wine quota system. | F | 121,078 | 39.9% | 182,724 | 60.1% |

## Montana Initiatives: 1976-1992 — continued

| Date | Code | No. | Ballot Proposition | Result | Yes Votes Number | Yes Votes Pct. | No Votes Number | No Votes Pct. |
|---|---|---|---|---|---|---|---|---|
| | | | **Direct Statutes — continued** | | | | | |
| (11/02/82) | bud | 95 | Invest Coal Tax Trust revenue in Montana economy. | P | 207,629 | 71.0% | 84,875 | 29.0% |
| 11/06/84 | oth | 96 | Milk price decontrol. | F | 145,342 | 39.5% | 222,200 | 60.5% |
| | oth | 97 | Allowing practice of Denturitry. | P | 194,285 | 53.1% | 171,448 | 46.9% |
| 11/04/86 | oth | 104 | Decontrol of milk prices. | F | 153,293 | 48.8% | 160,835 | 51.2% |
| | bud | 105 | Limit property taxes to 1986 levels. | P | 166,694 | 54.9% | 136,904 | 45.1% |
| 11/06/88 | oth | 110 | Repeal the Montana Seatbelt Use Act. | F | 155,481 | 42.4% | 211,090 | 57.6% |
| | bev | 113 | Refundable deposits on beverage containers. | F | 78,509 | 21.5% | 287,461 | 78.5% |
| 11/06/90 | bud | 115 | Increase cigarette sales tax. | F | 130,707 | 40.9% | 188,732 | 59.1% |
| | | | Total Attempted 20 | | | | | |
| | | | Total Passed 11 | | | | | |
| | | | **Memorial** | | | | | |
| 11/02/82 | nw | 91 | Opposing placement of MX Missiles in Montana. | P | 168,594 | 57.4% | 125,092 | 42.6% |
| | | | Total Attempted 1 | | | | | |
| | | | Total Passed 1 | | | | | |

## Nebraska Initiatives: 1976-1992

| Date | Code | No. | Ballot Proposition | Result | Yes Votes | | No Votes | |
|---|---|---|---|---|---|---|---|---|
| | | | | | Number | Pct. | Number | Pct. |
| | | | **Constitutional Amendments** | | | | | |
| 11/02/82 | oth | 300 | NE Family Farm Corporations must own farms. | P | 290,377 | 56.4% | 224,555 | 43.6% |
| 11/08/88 | cri | 403 | Right to bear arms. | P | 393,829 | 64.5% | 216,528 | 35.5% |
| 11/06/90 | lot | 404 | State lottery. | F | 202,814 | 35.3% | 371,711 | 64.7% |
| | bud | 405 | Limits budget appropriations. | F | 178,749 | 30.8% | 400,872 | 69.2% |
| 11/03/92 | ter | 407 | Term limits: State officers. | P | 481,048 | 68.2% | 224,114 | 31.8% |
| | | | Total Attempted 5 | | | | | |
| | | | Total Passed 3 | | | | | |
| | | | **Direct Statutes** | | | | | |
| 11/07/78 | bev | 301 | Five cent deposit: beverage containers. | F | 211,732 | 43.0% | 280,522 | 57.0% |
| | red | 302 | Five percent increase limit on political subdivisions. | F | 211,106 | 44.5% | 262,949 | 55.5% |
| 11/08/88 | np | 402 | Central Interstate Radioactive Waste Compact. | F | 225,174 | 35.2% | 414,394 | 64.8% |
| | | | Total Attempted 3 | | | | | |
| | | | Total Passed 0 | | | | | |

## Nevada Initiatives: 1976-1992

| Date | Code | No. | Ballot Proposition | Result | Yes Votes | | No Votes | |
|---|---|---|---|---|---|---|---|---|
| | | | | | Number | Pct. | Number | Pct. |
| | | | **Constitutional Amendments** | | | | | |
| 11/07/78 | | 6 | Limit property taxes. | P | 140,509 | 77.8% | 40,154 | 22.2% |
| 11/04/80 | bud | | 1978 Initiative #6. | F | 103,334 | 42.5% | 140,018 | 57.5% |
| | | 8 | Exempt household goods from taxation. | P | 178,947 | 77.3% | 52,593 | 22.7% |
| | | 9 | Exempt food from taxation. | P | 163,384 | 70.3% | 68,985 | 29.7% |
| 11/02/82 | bud | | 1980 Initiative #8. | P | 169,066 | 75.7% | 54,368 | 24.3% |
| | bud | | 1980 Initiative #9. | F | 94,014 | 41.2% | 133,999 | 58.8% |
| 11/06/84 | bud | 12 | Limit tax increases, all levels of government. | F | 132,688 | 48.0% | 143,874 | 52.0% |
| 11/08/88 | | 9 | Prohibit a State personal income tax. | P | 276,976 | 82.2% | 59,803 | 17.8% |
| 11/06/90 | bud | | 1988 Initiative #9. | P | 226,079 | 72.4% | 86,335 | 27.6% |
| | | | Total Attempted 5 | | | | | |
| | | | Total Passed 2 | | | | | |
| | | | **Indirect Statutes** | | | | | |
| 11/02/82 | uti | 12 | Protection of public utilities customers. | F | 93,502 | 42.8% | 124,964 | 57.2% |
| 11/06/90 | bud | 6 | Net profit tax, franchise fee for corporations. | F | 72,574 | 23.0% | 242,366 | 77.0% |
| | | | Total Attempted 2 | | | | | |
| | | | Total Passed 0 | | | | | |

## North Dakota Initiatives: 1976-1992

| Date | Code | No. | Ballot Proposition | Result | Yes Votes Number | Yes Votes Pct. | No Votes Number | No Votes Pct. |
|---|---|---|---|---|---|---|---|---|
| | | | **Constitutional Amendments** | | | | | |
| 11/06/84 | cri | 3 | Right to bear arms as a State right. | P | 236,596 | 80.2% | 58,582 | 19.8% |
| 06/14/88 | lot | | Legislative assembly to establish State lottery. | F | 43,951 | 41.7% | 61,331 | 58.3% |
| 11/06/90 | lot | | Games of chance: proceeds, Roland Township. | F | 73,649 | 32.1% | 155,534 | 67.9% |
| 11/06/90 | lot | | Electronic video gaming, proceeds. | F | 76,700 | 33.4% | 152,918 | 66.6% |
| | | | Total Attempted 4 | | | | | |
| | | | Total Passed 1 | | | | | |
| | | | **Direct Statutes** | | | | | |
| 09/07/76 | bud | IA9 | Limit General Fund expenditures, $332M. | F | 50,917 | 40.2% | 75,790 | 59.8% |
| 11/02/76 | bud | IA1 | Motor vehicle excise tax rates. | P | 145,499 | 57.8% | 106,341 | 42.2% |
| 11/07/78 | bud | IA13 | State sharing of General Fund revenues. | P | 146,187 | 72.0% | 56,761 | 28.0% |
| | bud | IA14 | Income tax rates: individual, corporate. | P | 127,280 | 65.1% | 68,215 | 34.9% |
| | bud | IA15 | Funds to Fish & Game Department. | P | 138,500 | 67.8% | 65,638 | 32.2% |
| | hea | IA16 | State control of health care costs, insurance. | F | 54,060 | 24.1% | 169,823 | 75.9% |
| 11/04/80 | bud | | 6.5% oil extraction tax, use of revenues. | P | 163,991 | 56.7% | 125,231 | 43.3% |
| | bud | | Tax-exempt bonds for low-income mortgages. | P | 159,633 | 60.4% | 104,644 | 39.6% |
| 11/02/82 | lot | 6 | Place limits on charitable gambling. | F | 96,677 | 37.0% | 164,816 | 63.0% |
| 11/06/84 | edu | 4 | Three junior colleges to local school board control. | F | 107,357 | 37.0% | 182,989 | 63.0% |
| 06/10/86 | oth | 4 | Sunday grocery employees: from six to three. | F | 57,903 | 46.2% | 67,544 | 53.8% |
| 11/04/86 | lot | 3 | Establish a State lottery. | F | 127,136 | 44.8% | 156,777 | 55.2% |
| | oth | | More businesses allowed open for retail on Sundays. | F | 115,422 | 40.1% | 172,577 | 59.9% |
| 11/08/88 | bud | | Restore Veterans' Postwar Trust Fund, 1987 balance. | P | 159,943 | 59.6% | 108,195 | 40.4% |
| 06/12/90 | bud | | Sales, use, motor vehicle taxes for education. | F | 52,610 | 41.5% | 74,207 | 58.5% |
| 11/06/90 | con | | Insurance agents can rebate their commission. | F | 25,825 | 11.4% | 201,326 | 88.6% |
| | lot | | Regulates private games of chance: video gaming. | F | 82,019 | 36.0% | 145,973 | 64.0% |

## North Dakota Initiatives: 1976-1992 — continued

| | | | | | Yes Votes | | No Votes | |
|---|---|---|---|---|---|---|---|---|
| Date | Code | No. | Ballot Proposition | Result | Number | Pct. | Number | Pct. |
| | | | **Direct Statutes — continued** | | | | | |
| 11/03/92 | bud | | Water development, sales and use tax. | F | 110,045 | 37.7% | 181,960 | 62.3% |
| | vot | | Ban write-in votes: U.S. Senator/Representative. | P | 162,150 | 55.5% | 129,930 | 44.5% |
| 11/03/92 | cri | | Prohibit stopping/searching vehicles at random. | F | 114,959 | 38.3% | 184,978 | 61.7% |
| | np | | Environmental protection fund, fees on waste. | F | 144,781 | 49.8% | 145,793 | 50.2% |
| | | | Total Attempted 21 | | | | | |
| | | | Total Passed 8 | | | | | |
| | | | **Memorial** | | | | | |
| 11/02/82 | nw | 7 | Limits: development/production of nuclear weapons. | P | 139,089 | 58.4% | 98,882 | 41.6% |
| | | | Total Attempted 1 | | | | | |
| | | | Total Passed 1 | | | | | |

## Ohio Initiatives: 1976-1992

| | | | | | Yes Votes | | No Votes | |
|---|---|---|---|---|---|---|---|---|
| Date | Code | No. | Ballot Proposition | Result | Number | Pct. | Number | Pct. |
| | | | **Constitutional Amendments** | | | | | |
| 11/02/76 | uti | 4 | Residential customers: gas, electricity rate limits. | F | 1,247,388 | 34.8% | 2,334,816 | 65.2% |
| | uti | 5 | Representation of utility consumers; regulation. | F | 1,092,781 | 29.9% | 2,557,265 | 70.1% |
| | np | 6 | Legislative approval of nuclear power facilities. | F | 1,150,360 | 31.8% | 2,462,000 | 68.2% |
| | vot | 7 | Simplifying procedures for initiative and referendum. | F | 1,175,410 | 32.8% | 2,407,960 | 67.2% |
| 11/08/77 | vot | | Entitlement to vote if registered for thirty (30) days. | P | 1,964,361 | 61.6% | 1,225,852 | 38.4% |
| | oth | | Ban trapping devices causing prolonged suffering. | F | 1,169,068 | 36.6% | 2,027,642 | 63.4% |
| 11/03/81 | con | 1 | Workers compensation insurance; private companies. | F | 572,227 | 20.9% | 2,164,395 | 79.1% |
| | red | 2 | General Assembly and Congressional redistricting. | F | 1,093,485 | 41.9% | 1,513,502 | 58.1% |
| 11/02/82 | uti | 3 | Election of members of Public Utilities Commission. | F | 1,053,274 | 32.6% | 2,175,893 | 67.4% |
| 11/08/83 | cri | 1 | Minimum age, beer consumption: twenty-one (21). | F | 1,386,959 | 41.4% | 1,965,469 | 58.6% |
| | bud | 2 | 3/5 majority of General Assembly to raise taxes. | F | 1,354,320 | 40.8% | 1,967,129 | 59.2% |
| | bud | 3 | Repeal all taxes passed since 1982. | F | 1,452,061 | 43.5% | 1,883,270 | 56.5% |
| 11/03/87 | vot | 3 | Abolish election of Supreme, Appeals Court judges. | F | 878,683 | 35.4% | 1,600,588 | 64.6% |
| 11/06/90 | lot | 3 | Casino resort hotel in Lorain as pilot project. | F | 1,270,387 | 37.7% | 2,098,725 | 62.3% |
| 11/02/92 | ter | 2 | Two successive term limit: U.S. Congress. | P | 2,897,123 | 66.2% | 1,476,461 | 33.8% |
| | ter | 3 | Term limits for State legislators. | P | 2,982,285 | 68.4% | 1,378,009 | 31.6% |
| | ter | 4 | Two successive terms for executive offices. | P | 3,028,288 | 69.2% | 1,349,244 | 30.8% |

Total Attempted 17
Total Passed 4

**Ohio Initiatives — continued**

| Date | Code | No. | Ballot Proposition | Result | Yes Votes Number | Yes Votes Pct. | No Votes Number | No Votes Pct. |
|---|---|---|---|---|---|---|---|---|
| | | | **Indirect Statutes** | | | | | |
| 11/06/79 | bev | 1 | Mandatory deposits on bottles; prohibit pull-tabs. | F | 768,898 | 27.6% | 2,019,834 | 72.4% |
| 11/02/92 | np | 5 | Businesses to provide warnings for toxic substances. | F | 1,007,882 | 21.9% | 3,587,734 | 78.1% |
| | | | Total Attempted 2 | | | | | |
| | | | Total Passed 0 | | | | | |

## Oklahoma Initiatives: 1976-1992

| Date | Code | No. | Ballot Proposition | Result | Yes Votes Number | Yes Votes Pct. | No Votes Number | No Votes Pct. |
|---|---|---|---|---|---|---|---|---|
| | | | **Constitutional Amendments** | | | | | |
| 11/02/76 | oth | 295 | Sale of alcoholic beverages, licensees, terms. | F | 483,832 | 46.5% | 556,401 | 53.5% |
| 09/18/84 | oth | 319 | Renaming Alcoholic Beverage Commission; taxation. | P | 425,803 | 51.8% | 396,923 | 48.2% |
| 03/14/89 | red | 339 | Legislative Session: dates and times. | P | 136,930 | 75.3% | 44,872 | 24.7% |
| 09/18/90 | oth | 341 | Create five-member Ethics Commission. | P | 409,100 | 63.8% | 231,899 | 36.2% |
| | ter | 346 | Legislative term limits: twelve years. | P | 437,806 | 67.3% | 213,158 | 32.7% |
| 03/10/92 | bud | 348 | Revenue bills approval: voters or 3/4 Legisl. + Gov. | P | 373,143 | 56.2% | 290,978 | 43.8% |
| | | | Total Attempted | 6 | | | | |
| | | | Total Passed | 5 | | | | |
| | | | **Direct Statutes** | | | | | |
| 11/07/78 | bud | 300 | License/registration through mail; Tax Commission. | P | 449,516 | 64.0% | 252,820 | 36.0% |
| 11/06/79 | bud | 309 | Deduct individual Fed. income tax from State income. | F | 202,380 | 48.9% | 211,768 | 51.1% |
| 09/21/82 | lot | 315 | Creation of Oklahoma Horse Racing Commission. | P | 449,124 | 58.1% | 324,550 | 41.9% |
| 11/02/82 | red | 317 | Creation of new Congressional districts. | F | 379,545 | 48.9% | 397,142 | 51.1% |
| 10/15/91 | edu | 347 | Repeal minimum standards for school accreditation. | F | 360,318 | 45.7% | 428,680 | 54.3% |
| | | | Total Attempted | 5 | | | | |
| | | | Total Passed | 2 | | | | |

## Oregon Initiatives: 1976-1992

| Date | Code | No. | Ballot Proposition | Result | Yes Votes Number | Yes Votes Pct. | No Votes Number | No Votes Pct. |
|---|---|---|---|---|---|---|---|---|
| | | | **Constitutional Amendments** | | | | | |
| 11/07/78 | bud | 6 | Limitations on ad valorem property taxes. | F | 424,029 | 48.3% | 453,741 | 51.7% |
| | abo | 7 | Prohibits State spending or programs for abortions. | F | 431,577 | 48.3% | 461,542 | 51.7% |
| | oth | 10 | Land use planning, zoning amendment. | F | 334,523 | 39.4% | 515,138 | 60.6% |
| 11/04/80 | bud | 6 | Property tax limit: 85% districts' 1977 revenue. | F | 416,029 | 36.9% | 711,617 | 63.1% |
| 11/02/82 | bud | 3 | Property tax limit: 85% districts' 1979 revenue. | F | 504,836 | 49.5% | 515,626 | 50.5% |
| 11/06/84 | bud | 2 | Property tax limit. | F | 599,424 | 49.3% | 616,252 | 50.7% |
| | lot | 4 | State lottery; profits for economic development. | P | 794,441 | 65.8% | 412,341 | 34.2% |
| | cri | 6 | Death penalty exempt: guarantees against cruelty. | P | 653,009 | 55.6% | 521,687 | 44.4% |
| 11/04/86 | abo | 6 | Prohibits State funding of abortions; exceptions. | F | 477,920 | 45.2% | 580,163 | 54.8% |
| | bud | 7 | Sales tax. Funds schools, reduces property taxes. | F | 234,804 | 22.3% | 816,369 | 77.7% |
| | bud | 9 | Limit property tax rate, assessed value increases. | F | 449,548 | 43.5% | 584,396 | 56.5% |
| | vot | 13 | Twenty day pre-election voter registration cutoff. | P | 693,460 | 66.9% | 343,450 | 33.1% |
| 11/06/90 | bud | 5 | Property tax limit; schools, government operations. | P | 574,833 | 52.4% | 522,022 | 47.6% |
| | abo | 8 | Prohibit abortion; exceptions. | F | 355,963 | 32.3% | 747,599 | 67.7% |
| | edu | 11 | Choice of public schools; tax credit, private schools. | F | 351,977 | 32.2% | 741,863 | 67.8% |
| 11/03/92 | ter | 3 | Term limits: State and Congressional legislators. | P | 1,003,706 | 69.5% | 439,694 | 30.5% |
| | bud | 7 | Raises limit on property tax; renters' tax relief. | F | 362,621 | 25.2% | 1,077,206 | 74.8% |
| | sex | 9 | Government to discourage homosexual "behaviors." | F | 638,527 | 43.5% | 828,290 | 56.5% |
| | | | Total Attempted 18 | | | | | |
| | | | Total Passed 5 | | | | | |
| | | | **Direct Statutes** | | | | | |
| 11/02/76 | np | 9 | Regulate approval, nuclear power plant construction. | F | 423,008 | 42.0% | 584,845 | 58.0% |
| | oth | 10 | Repeal of land use planning coordination statutes. | F | 402,608 | 42.9% | 536,502 | 57.1% |
| | oth | 11 | Prohibit adding fluoridation to water systems. | F | 419,567 | 43.0% | 555,981 | 57.0% |

## Oregon Initiatives: 1976-1992 — continued

| Date | Code | No. | Ballot Proposition | Result | Yes Votes | | No Votes | |
|---|---|---|---|---|---|---|---|---|
| | | | | | Number | Pct. | Number | Pct. |
| | | | **Direct Statutes — continued** | | | | | |
| (11/02/76) | oth | 12 | Repeal intergovernmental cooperation, planning. | F | 333,933 | 38.8% | 525,868 | 61.2% |
| 11/07/78 | uti | 4 | Shorten formation procedures: utility districts. | F | 375,587 | 44.4% | 471,027 | 55.6% |
| | oth | 5 | Practice of denture technology. | P | 704,480 | 77.8% | 201,463 | 22.2% |
| | cri | 8 | Death penalty for murder, specific conditions. | P | 573,707 | 64.3% | 318,610 | 35.7% |
| | uti | 9 | Limit public utility rate base. | P | 589,361 | 68.8% | 267,132 | 31.2% |
| 11/04/80 | oth | 5 | Forbid use, sale of snare leghold traps. | F | 425,890 | 36.9% | 728,173 | 63.1% |
| | np | 7 | Nuclear plant licensing: voter approval, disposal. | P | 608,412 | 53.2% | 535,049 | 46.8% |
| 11/02/82 | oth | 4 | Permit retail self-service dispensing of fuel. | F | 440,824 | 42.4% | 597,970 | 57.6% |
| | oth | 6 | End State's land use planning powers; localities. | F | 461,271 | 44.9% | 565,056 | 55.1% |
| 11/06/84 | uti | 3 | Citizens' utility board. | P | 637,968 | 53.4% | 556,826 | 46.6% |
| | lot | 5 | Statutory provisions for State operated lottery. | P | 786,933 | 66.3% | 399,231 | 33.7% |
| | cri | 7 | Death/mandatory imprisonment: aggravated murder. | P | 893,818 | 75.1% | 295,988 | 24.9% |
| | cri | 8 | Criminal laws: police powers, evidence, sentences. | F | 552,410 | 48.0% | 597,964 | 52.0% |
| | np | 9 | Naturally occurring radioactive isotopes: disposal. | P | 655,973 | 55.6% | 524,214 | 44.4% |
| 11/04/86 | cri | 5 | Legalize marijuana for personal use. | F | 279,479 | 26.3% | 781,922 | 73.7% |
| | uti | 8 | Mandatory local measured telephone service. | P | 802,099 | 79.9% | 201,918 | 20.1% |
| | cri | 10 | Criminal laws: victims, evidence, sentences, parole. | P | 774,766 | 75.5% | 251,509 | 24.5% |
| | bud | 11 | Property tax relief program; sales tax limitation. | F | 381,727 | 37.4% | 639,034 | 62.6% |
| | bud | 12 | State income tax changes, property tax relief. | F | 299,551 | 29.4% | 720,034 | 70.6% |
| | np | 14 | Nuclear Power: permanent waste site licensed. | F | 375,241 | 35.7% | 674,641 | 64.3% |
| | np | 15 | "Radioactive waste" defined; energy facility payments. | F | 424,099 | 43.2% | 558,741 | 56.8% |
| | nw | 16 | Nuclear weapons funded by tax credits. Civil penalty. | F | 400,119 | 40.4% | 590,971 | 59.6% |
| 11/08/88 | cri | 4 | Full sentences, no parole; probation, repeat felonies. | P | 947,805 | 78.9% | 252,985 | 21.1% |
| | bud | 5 | Sin taxes to finance Intercollegiate Athletic Fund. | F | 449,797 | 37.2% | 759,360 | 62.8% |
| | oth | 6 | Indoor Clean Air Law revisions: ban public smoking. | F | 480,147 | 39.4% | 737,779 | 60.6% |
| | oth | 7 | Oregon Scenic Waterway System: river sections. | P | 663,604 | 56.2% | 516,998 | 43.8% |
| | sex | 8 | Revoke ban on sexual orientation discrimination. | P | 626,751 | 52.8% | 561,355 | 47.2% |

**Oregon Initiatives: 1976-1992 — continued**

| Date | Code | No. | Ballot Proposition | Result | Yes Votes Number | Yes Votes Pct. | No Votes Number | No Votes Pct. |
|---|---|---|---|---|---|---|---|---|
| | | | **Direct Statutes — continued** | | | | | |
| 11/06/90 | np | 4 | Prohibit Trojan operation until standards met. | F | 446,795 | 40.3% | 660,992 | 59.7% |
| | bev | 6 | Product packaging: recycling, hardship waivers. | F | 467,418 | 42.3% | 636,804 | 57.7% |
| | bud | 7 | Work in lieu of Welfare benefits pilot program. | P | 624,744 | 58.0% | 452,853 | 42.0% |
| | oth | 9 | Requires use of safety belts. | P | 598,460 | 53.9% | 512,872 | 46.1% |
| | abo | 10 | Parental notice before minor's abortion. | F | 530,851 | 47.9% | 577,806 | 52.1% |
| 11/03/92 | oth | 4 | Ban triple truck-trailers on Oregon highways. | F | 567,467 | 38.8% | 896,778 | 61.2% |
| | np | 5 | Close Trojan: waste, cost, and earthquake orders. | F | 585,051 | 40.1% | 874,636 | 59.9% |
| | np | 6 | Bans Trojan operation unless conditions met. | F | 619,329 | 42.7% | 830,850 | 57.3% |
| | oth | 8 | Lower Columbia fish harvests. | F | 576,633 | 41.0% | 828,096 | 59.0% |
| | | | Total Attempted 39 | | | | | |
| | | | Total Passed 15 | | | | | |
| | | | **Memorial** | | | | | |
| 11/02/82 | nw | 5 | Mutual freeze on nuclear weapons development. | P | 623,089 | 61.6% | 387,907 | 38.4% |
| | | | Total Attempted 1 | | | | | |
| | | | Total Passed 1 | | | | | |

## South Dakota Initiatives: 1976-1992

| Date | Code | No. | Ballot Proposition | Result | Yes Votes | | No Votes | |
|---|---|---|---|---|---|---|---|---|
| | | | | | Number | Pct. | Number | Pct. |
| | | | **Constitutional Amendments** | | | | | |
| 11/04/80 | bud | B | Relating to real property taxes. | F | 113,863 | 37.2% | 192,116 | 62.8% |
| 11/04/80 | vot | C | Legislature cannot change initiative-enacted laws. | F | 126,181 | 47.3% | 140,632 | 52.7% |
| 11/02/82 | red | A | Single member senate districts in legislature. | P | 122,703 | 52.2% | 112,184 | 47.8% |
| 11/08/88 | lot | B | Permit gambling in city of Deadwood. | P | 191,745 | 64.3% | 106,444 | 35.7% |
| | bud | C | Add section limiting property taxes. | F | 116,240 | 38.7% | 184,452 | 61.3% |
| 11/03/92 | ter | A | Term limitations. | P | 205,074 | 63.5% | 117,702 | 36.5% |
| | | | Total Attempted 6 | | | | | |
| | | | Total Passed 3 | | | | | |
| | | | **Indirect Statutes** | | | | | |
| 11/07/78 | uti | IA5 | Lifeline utility rate reform. | F | 91,707 | 39.4% | 140,899 | 60.6% |
| | oth | IA6 | Repeal of Dairy Marketing Act. | P | 120,813 | 52.5% | 109,109 | 47.5% |
| | cri | IA7 | New regulation of Obscenity Statute. | F | 60,051 | 25.4% | 176,152 | 74.6% |
| 11/04/80 | np | 2 | Uranium, nuclear waste, plants: voter approval. | F | 146,381 | 48.4% | 156,293 | 51.6% |
| 11/06/84 | np | 1 | Voter approval: nuclear waste disposal, compacts. | P | 182,952 | 62.0% | 112,161 | 38.0% |
| | edu | 2 | School begins day after Labor Day. | P | 145,472 | 50.1% | 144,908 | 49.9% |
| 11/04/86 | oth | 1 | Memorial Day observed last monday in May. | P | 164,732 | 58.5% | 117,063 | 41.5% |
| 11/08/88 | oth | 1 | Surface mining reclamation. | F | 123,738 | 40.5% | 181,729 | 59.5% |
| | bud | 2 | Additional tax on surface mining. | F | 105,859 | 35.1% | 196,037 | 64.9% |
| | oth | 3 | Ban on corporate hog farms. | P | 178,955 | 59.7% | 120,605 | 40.3% |
| 11/06/90 | np | 1 | Legislative approval: large scale waste facilities. | P | 130,465 | 53.0% | 115,894 | 47.0% |
| | oth | 2 | Permits for large scale gold/silver mining. | F | 116,583 | 47.3% | 129,824 | 52.7% |

## South Dakota Initiatives: 1976-1992 — continued

| Date | Code | No. | Ballot Proposition | Result | Yes Votes Number | Yes Votes Pct. | No Votes Number | No Votes Pct. |
|---|---|---|---|---|---|---|---|---|
| | | | **Indirect Statues — continued** | | | | | |
| 11/03/92 | oth | 2 | Regulation, reclamation: gold/silver mining. | P | 189,683 | 59.7% | 128,109 | 40.3% |
| | bud | 3 | Various tax reductions, redistribution. | F | 80,171 | 25.4% | 235,871 | 74.6% |
| | lot | 4 | Repeal the video lottery. | F | 122,298 | 37.1% | 207,607 | 62.9% |
| | | | Total Attempted 15 | | | | | |
| | | | Total Passed 7 | | | | | |
| | | | **Memorial** | | | | | |
| 11/06/84 | nw | 3 | SD mandates a verifiable nuclear freeze. | F | 135,307 | 47.6% | 148,705 | 52.4% |
| | | | Total Attempted 1 | | | | | |
| | | | Total Passed 0 | | | | | |

## Utah Initiatives: 1976-1992

| Date | Code | No. | Ballot Proposition | Result | Yes Votes | | No Votes | |
|---|---|---|---|---|---|---|---|---|
| | | | | | Number | Pct. | Number | Pct. |
| | | | **Direct Statutes** | | | | | |
| 11/02/76 | oth | A | Freedom from compulsory fluoridation/medication. | P | 262,416 | 50.1% | 261,262 | 49.9% |
| | red | B | Utah recall and advisory recall act. | F | 254,865 | 49.8% | 257,246 | 50.2% |
| | bud | C | Budget ceiling initiative. | F | 112,414 | 22.2% | 394,762 | 77.8% |
| 11/04/80 | bud | A | Elimination of sales tax on food. | F | 256,075 | 44.1% | 324,555 | 55.9% |
| | bud | B | Tax limitation act. | F | 258,749 | 45.2% | 313,329 | 54.8% |
| 11/06/84 | oth | A | Cable television decency act. | F | 238,734 | 39.0% | 373,361 | 61.0% |
| 11/08/88 | bud | A | Tax and spending limitations. | F | 242,883 | 38.6% | 386,098 | 61.4% |
| | bud | B | Tax reductions. | F | 239,284 | 38.0% | 390,627 | 62.0% |
| | bud | C | Income tax credit for private education. | F | 190,193 | 30.2% | 439,090 | 69.8% |
| 11/06/90 | bud | A | Removal of state, local sales tax from food. | F | 194,448 | 44.2% | 245,045 | 55.8% |
| 11/03/92 | lot | A | State-regulated horse races; pari-mutual wagering. | F | 297,542 | 39.7% | 451,517 | 60.3% |

Total Attempted 11
Total Passed 1

## Washington Initiatives: 1976-1992

| Date | Code | No. | Ballot Proposition | Result | Yes Votes | | No Votes | |
|---|---|---|---|---|---|---|---|---|
| | | | | | Number | Pct. | Number | Pct. |
| | | | **Direct Statutes** | | | | | |
| 11/02/76 | oth | 322 | Fluoridation of public water: unlawful, penalty. | F | 469,929 | 35.1% | 870,631 | 64.9% |
| | np | 325 | Nuclear power facilities: 2/3 vote in legislature. | F | 482,953 | 33.4% | 963,756 | 66.6% |
| 11/08/77 | oth | 335 | Regulation of pornography. | P | 522,921 | 54.8% | 431,989 | 45.2% |
| | bud | 345 | State, local sales and use taxes: food exemptions. | P | 521,062 | 54.0% | 443,840 | 46.0% |
| | bud | 348 | Repeal of variable fuel tax. | F | 470,147 | 50.0% | 471,031 | 50.0% |
| 11/07/78 | edu | 350 | Assignment of students to schools: prohibitions. | P | 585,903 | 66.3% | 297,991 | 33.7% |
| 11/04/80 | np | 383 | Bans on radioactive wastes generated out of State. | P | 1,211,606 | 75.5% | 393,415 | 24.5% |
| 11/03/81 | bud | 394 | Voter approval: bonds for public energy projects. | P | 532,178 | 58.1% | 384,419 | 41.9% |
| | bud | 402 | Abolition of State inheritance and gift tax. | P | 610,507 | 67.2% | 297,445 | 32.8% |
| 11/02/82 | oth | 412 | Maximum interest rate on retail sales. | F | 452,710 | 34.0% | 880,135 | 66.0% |
| | bev | 414 | Five cent refund on beverage containers. | F | 400,156 | 29.3% | 965,951 | 70.7% |
| | bud | 435 | Sales, other business taxes replaced by franchise tax. | F | 453,221 | 33.8% | 889,091 | 66.2% |
| 11/06/84 | bud | 464 | Trade-in values; sales tax computation. | P | 1,175,781 | 68.9% | 529,560 | 31.1% |
| | abo | 471 | No public funding of abortions; exceptions. | F | 838,083 | 46.9% | 949,921 | 53.1% |
| 11/08/88 | oth | 518 | Minimum wage increases: include agricultural sector. | P | 1,354,454 | 76.5% | 414,926 | 23.5% |
| 11/06/90 | oth | 547 | Growth and environmental protection goals, fees. | F | 327,339 | 24.9% | 986,505 | 75.1% |
| 11/05/91 | ter | 553 | Term limitations: State and federal officers. | F | 690,828 | 46.0% | 811,686 | 54.0% |
| | bud | 559 | Adjust property value for tax purposes. | F | 592,391 | 40.5% | 869,626 | 59.5% |
| 11/03/92 | ter | 573 | Limit tenure in office through ballot access. | P | 1,119,985 | 52.4% | 1,018,260 | 47.6% |

Total Attempted 19
Total Passed 9

## Washington Initiatives: 1976-1992 — continued

| Date | Code | No. | Ballot Proposition | Result | Yes Votes | | No Votes | |
|---|---|---|---|---|---|---|---|---|
| | | | | | Number | Pct. | Number | Pct. |
| | | | **Indirect Statutes** | | | | | |
| 11/08/77 | oth | 59 | Limit appropriations of public water: agriculture. | P | 457,054 | 51.1% | 437,682 | 48.9% |
| 11/06/79 | bev | 61 | Five cent refund on beverage containers. | F | 380,247 | 42.4% | 517,177 | 57.6% |
| | bud | 62 | State tax revenue limitation. | P | 588,724 | 68.3% | 272,761 | 31.7% |
| 11/04/86 | bud | 90 | Sales/use tax for conservation, recreation programs. | F | 493,794 | 38.6% | 784,382 | 61.4% |
| 11/03/87 | hea | 92 | Charges to Medicare patients; reasonable charges. | F | 315,792 | 35.5% | 572,813 | 64.5% |
| 11/08/88 | | 97 | Waste cleanup: part-funded by 0.7% hazardous substance tax. | | | | | |
| | | 97b | Legislative cleanup program: 0.8% hazardous substance tax. | | | | | |
| | np | | For either / Against both | P | 1,307,638 | 85.3% | 224,486 | 14.7% |
| | np | | For 97 / For 97B | P | 860,835 | 56.0% | 676,469 | 44.0% |
| 06/11/05 | bud | 102 | $360K new taxes for family services, K-12 education. | F | 349,357 | 33.7% | 688,782 | 66.3% |
| 11/05/91 | oth | 119 | Allow terminally ill adults: physician aid-in-dying. | F | 701,808 | 46.4% | 810,623 | 53.6% |
| | abo | 120 | Revise abortion laws: a woman's right to choose. | P | 756,812 | 50.1% | 752,590 | 49.9% |
| 11/03/92 | cam | 134 | Limit campaign contributions, funding, campaigns. | P | 1,549,297 | 72.9% | 576,161 | 27.1% |
| | | | Total Attempted 11 | | | | | |
| | | | Total Passed 6 | | | | | |
| | | | **Memorial** | | | | | |
| 11/06/84 | oth | 456 | Petition Congress to decommercialize steelhead. | P | 916,855 | 53.2% | 807,825 | 46.8% |
| | | | Total Attempted 1 | | | | | |
| | | | Total Passed 1 | | | | | |

## Wyoming Initiatives: 1976-1992

| Date | Code | No. | Ballot Proposition | Result | Yes Votes Number | Yes Votes Pct. | No Votes Number | No Votes Pct. |
|---|---|---|---|---|---|---|---|---|
| | | | **Direct Statutes** | | | | | |
| 11/03/92 | oth | 1 | Ban triple trailers from State highways. | P | 165,879 | 83.8% | 31,997 | 16.2% |
| | ter | 2 | Term limits: State and federal officials. | P | 150,113 | 77.2% | 44,424 | 22.8% |
| | np | 3 | Railroads: emergencies, toxics, hazardous materials. | P | 130,803 | 71.2% | 52,835 | 28.8% |
| | | | Total Attempted 3 | | | | | |
| | | | Total Passed 3 | | | | | |

# APPENDIX A

## Summary of Initiative Activity Prior to 1976

| State | Type of Initiative | Passed | Failed | Total |
|---|---|---|---|---|
| **Alaska** | Statutes | 2 | 2 | 4 |
| **Arizona** | Const. Amendments | 19 | 27 | 46 |
| | Statutes | 23 | 42 | 65 |
| | Total | 42 | 69 | 111 |
| **Arkansas** | Const. Amendments | 30 | 16 | 46 |
| | Statutes | 8 | 9 | 17 |
| | Total | 38 | 25 | 63 |
| **California** | Const. Amendments | 24 | 65 | 89 |
| | Directs Statutes | 16 | 42 | 58 |
| | Indirect Statutes | 1 | 3 | 4 |
| | Bonds | 1 | 1 | 2 |
| | Total | 42 | 111 | 153 |
| **Colorado** | Const. Amendments | 21 | 48 | 69 |
| | Statutes | 20 | 25 | 45 |
| | Total | 41 | 73 | 114 |
| **Florida** | Const. Amendments | 0 | 0 | 0 |
| **Idaho** | Statutes | 5 | 6 | 11 |
| **Illinois** | Const. Amendments | 0 | 0 | 0 |
| **Maine** | Indirect Statutes | 3 | 8 | 11 |
| **Massachusetts** | Indirect Const. Amendments | 2 | 0 | 2 |
| | Indirect Statutes | 12 | 10 | 22 |
| | Total | 14 | 10 | 24 |
| **Michigan** | Const. Amendments | 9 | 23 | 32 |
| | Indirect Statutes | 2 | 1 | 3 |
| | Total | 11 | 24 | 35 |
| **Missouri** | Const. Amendments | 6 | 21 | 27 |
| | Statutes | 4 | 9 | 13 |
| | Total | 10 | 30 | 40 |
| **Montana** | Const. Amendments | 1 | 0 | 1 |
| | Statutes | 13 | 10 | 23 |
| | Total | 14 | 10 | 24 |

| | | | | |
|---|---|---|---|---|
| **Nebraska** | Const. Amendments | 7 | 8 | 15 |
| | Statutes | 1 | 8 | 9 |
| | Total | 8 | 16 | 24 |
| **Nevada** | Const. Amendments | 2 | 1 | 3 |
| | Indirect Statutes | 5 | 7 | 12 |
| | Total | 7 | 8 | 15 |
| **North Dakota** | Const. Amendments | 12 | 11 | 23 |
| | Indirect Const. Amendments | 7 | 0 | 7 |
| | Statutes | 43 | 61 | 104 |
| | Total | 62 | 72 | 134 |
| **Ohio** | Const. Amendments | 9 | 25 | 34 |
| | Indirect Statutes | 2 | 4 | 6 |
| | Total | 11 | 29 | 40 |
| **Oklahoma** | Const. Amendments | 10 | 33 | 43 |
| | Statutes | 6 | 20 | 26 |
| | Total | 16 | 53 | 69 |
| **Oregon** | Const. Amendments | 30 | 58 | 88 |
| | Statutes | 39 | 75 | 114 |
| | Total | 69 | 133 | 202 |
| **South Dakota** | Indirect Statutes | 2 | 17 | 19 |
| **Utah** | Statutes | 1 | 2 | 3 |
| **Washington** | Statutes | 33 | 34 | 67 |
| | Indirect Statutes | 6 | 3 | 9 |
| | Total | 39 | 37 | 76 |
| **Wyoming** | Statutes | 0 | 0 | 0 |
| **TOTAL** | | 453 | 719 | 1172 |

# INDEX

## E



## F



## G



## H



## I